HOUSE OF
SEVEN PATHS

PISTIS

THE ART OF TRUSTING THE UNSEEN

SAMANDA LEROY

Copyright © 2025 Samanda Leroy
First Edition, 2025

All rights reserved. Except for brief quotations in review or references, no part of this book may be reproduced, stored in a retrieval system, or transmitted in any form or by any means—electronic, mechanical, photocopying, recording, or otherwise—without prior written permission from the publisher.

All quotations from copyrighted works are reprinted under fair-use guidelines for critique and commentary. Every effort has been made to trace sources; any inadvertent omissions will be rectified in later editions.

This publication may contain references to trademarked names and products. All trademarks are the property of their respective owners. The use of such trademarks herein is for editorial purposes only and does not constitute endorsement or sponsorship. No trademark infringement is intended.

Scripture quotations taken from The Holy Bible, New International Version® NIV® Copyright © 1973, 1978, 1984, 2011 by Biblica, Inc
Used with permission. All rights reserved worldwide.

This is a non-fiction work based on the author's personal experiences and insights. The author makes no claims to provide medical, legal, or psychological advice. Readers are encouraged to use their own discernment.

ISBNs
Paperback: 979-8-9993080-0-9
Hardcover: 979-8-9993080-1-6
e-book: 979-8-9993080-2-3

Published by House of Seven Paths
Orlando, FL, USA.

For permissions, inquiries, or speaking engagements, contact House of Seven Paths at: info@houseofsevenpaths.com

To those who listen to the quiet voice within:
you were never lost. You were always being led.
There is a knowing before thought, and a
light before time.
It was not born, it simply is.
It will not end, it simply becomes.
You carry it in your silence, and it carries you in
every step.

"What we seek has never been lost. It has only been hidden behind the noise we were taught to believe."
—Samanda Leroy

CONTENTS

PREFACE 9
INTRODUCTION 11

PART I 15
Chapter 1 The Whisper That Knew Me 17
Chapter 2 Trusting the Unseen Is Trusting Yourself 25
Chapter 3 The Source of Many Voices, but One Origin ... 43
Chapter 4 The Lie of Holy Perfection 59
Chapter 5 The Three Realms of Being 71
Chapter 6 The Illusion of Separation 83
Chapter 7 The Sacred Law of Diversity 91

PART II 99
INTRODUCTION 101
Chapter 8 The Divine Mirror 103
Chapter 9 The Principle of Forgiveness 117
Chapter 10 Listening for the Sacred Yes 127
Chapter 11 Dreams: Conversations Between Realms 137
Chapter 12 The Line Between Life and Death 147
Chapter 13 When Words Become Home 157
Chapter 14 Manifestation: Power Guided by the Soul 167

PART III 179
INTRODUCTION 181
Chapter 15 Boundaries as Spiritual Tool 183
Chapter 16 The Practice of Being Present..................................... 191
Chapter 17 The Wisdom of Silence.. 199
Chapter 18 Embracing the Flow of Gratitude 207
Chapter 19 When the Spirit Leads 217
Chapter 20 The Dance Between Destiny and Free Will 223
Chapter 21 The Return to Light... 231

EPILOGUE 235
ACKNOWLEDGMENTS 236
ABOUT THE AUTHOR 238
REFERENCES AND RECOMMENDED READING................. 239

PREFACE

Before we begin, I want to thank you for being here. Your time, your presence, and your openness mean more than you know.

I want to take this moment to let you know that I did not write this book because I had all the answers; rather, because I had questions that would not let me go. I wrote it because there were moments in my life when I felt something holding me up when everything around me was falling apart. I did not always understand it, but I knew it was real, and that is where my trust and relationship with the *unseen* began.

If you are holding this book, something inside you is probably nudging you as well. However, this is not a book of rules. It is not a manual for perfection. It is a companion for the moments when you feel lost and unheard, when you question your path, or when life feels louder than your soul.

You will not find formulas here. You will find honesty—stories and questions that invite you back to wisdom, I believe, you have always carried.

This journey comes in three stages: remembering who you are, aligning with *your* truth, and embodying the spiritual in daily life so that you can deepen your relationship with yourself, with others, and by extension, with the unseen forces that govern life.

I wrote this book to remember who I am and to offer you a mirror for the same revelation. If anything on these pages helps you in any way, then every word has done its work.

Let this book be what it needs to be for you. A whisper. A mirror. A pause. A beginning. And above all, take your time. Your spirit is not in a hurry.

With love and presence,
—Samanda Leroy

INTRODUCTION
An Invitation to the Unseen.

Have you ever felt something guiding you, protecting you, whispering to you when the world was silent?

Maybe it came during a walk when the trees felt like they were breathing with you. Maybe it was during a heartbreak when something deep inside said, *"You will be fine."* Or perhaps it was just a moment—barely noticeable—when you were silent and sensed you were being watched over.

If you have ever felt guided, protected, loved, blessed, and cared for by something higher than yourself, this book has found you at the right time. That sense of invisible companionship, of being watched over even in silence is *real*, and you are not alone.

The ancient word *pistis* comes from Greek and early spiritual texts. It means faith, divine trust, and inner knowing that transcends logic.

More than belief, *pistis* is the sacred thread that connects us to the unknown—even when nothing makes sense.

This is not a religious book. Though it may reference texts or share stories rooted in my upbringing; this is not about doctrine. It is about *resonance*. Resonance is what you feel when something unspoken aligns deeply with your inner knowing. It is the *truth* whispered to you when no one else is around, and the way life moves when you start trusting the voice within.

I am not writing from a place of perfection. I am writing from experience, from inner voices, synchronicities, and dreams that taught me that *life is not random.*

There is guidance, even when we cannot explain it. There is purpose, even in pain; and there is a path, even when you cannot yet see where it leads.

For over a decade, I walked in quite a different direction. I graduated from law school and spent many years working in the legal industry. When I moved to the United States, I continued this journey as an immigration paralegal, and later as a litigation paralegal in a national law firm.

I was passionate, driven, and genuinely loved the work I was doing, but something began to stir within me; something that had been there for a very long time, something that had always found its way to me.

It was a persistent inner voice.

At first, it was just a whisper: *"It is time."*

Then it became louder: *"Now is the time."*

It did not come from fear or fatigue. It came from a deeper place—one I could not ignore. Eventually, I surrendered.

I did not know what would happen next. I had no clear plan, but I knew I had to listen. So, I quit my job and everything changed.

Since that moment, I have been guided in ways I cannot fully explain: books started appearing in my life; teachings found me at just the right time, and most clearly of all—I was told to write.

Writing this book is not just a creative project; it feels like a command from something greater than myself—something that made it clear I am no longer building a career, but stepping into a calling. This book is the result of that trust.

Pistis is the unfolding of my spiritual journey;

INTRODUCTION

from a sick child to a driven woman seeking success, and finally to a soul remembering her purpose. Along the way, I encountered moments that defied logic, voices that protected me, losses that transformed me, and signs that taught me that *faith is more than belief—it is a way of understanding.*

I share my story not because I believe I am different, but because I know I am not. I believe that we are all guided, but most of us were never taught how to listen.

This book is an invitation to remember who you are beneath the roles and identities, to explore what guidance feels like in your own life, and to trust that what brought you here will carry you further than you ever imagined.

What if every closed door, every inexplicable hunch, and every sudden swell of wonder you have ever felt were clues from an invisible compass already pointing you home? This book is an invitation to follow that barely audible guidance—the breeze beneath the noise—and to discover what waits when certainty loosens its grip and something larger is given the lead.

To write this book, I blend timeless principles and the universal law of love, not as rigid doctrine, but as living signposts—reminders that our personal awakening is inseparable from learning to live and love one another in harmony with our highest selves, and with the forces and orders that exist both within and beyond us.

As you read, pause whenever a sentence shimmers, and let the page become your listening room. Scattered throughout the chapters, you will find short parables, reflection prompts, and simple acts of presence. Use them as turning mirrors: breathe with the words, jot a line in the margin, close your eyes and feel what stirs.

Understanding and transformation are not delivered by ink alone; they arrive when you give the text room to speak through your own life. Treat these pages as a living dialogue, and they will answer you in ways no author could script.

You do not need to agree with everything in these pages. You only need to stay open to the possibility that you are more powerful, more connected, and more supported than you have been told. This is my invitation to you to walk the path of inner knowing.

You are being guided. This is your confirmation. Welcome.

PART I

IDENTITY THROUGH THE LENS OF THE SOUL

Focus: remember your true self, your divine origin, and inner guidance.

PISTIS: The Art of Trusting the Unseen

CHAPTER 1

THE WHISPER THAT KNEW ME

Let me start by introducing myself. You surely have read my name on the cover of this book, but I do not believe that my name alone describes who I am.

Perhaps, as you read these pages, you will find something about me that reminds you of yourself. And maybe—just maybe—you will begin to see life with the same quiet hope and peace that I feel today.

To be fully transparent with you, let me take you through a summary of my life's journey:

I was born and raised in Haiti and moved to the United States at the age of twenty-eight. For a long time, I described myself through labels: an immigrant, a Black woman, an independent person. I wore those identities with pride and intention. I wanted the world to see someone strong, someone breaking stereotypes.

In truth, I was trying to rewrite how the world perceived people *like me*. I was surrounded by external noise and expectations, and I let them shape the way I presented myself.

I, therefore, built an identity that made sense to the world: resilient, determined, educated. But beneath it all, something deeper was always whispering—reminding me that none of these labels were enough to define who I truly am.

Today, I can confidently say:

"I am spirit clothed in form, walking this earth for a purpose greater than I can see. I trust that my path is aligned not only with my highest good, but with the unfolding of all. I carry light—not as something I shine, but as something I remember. I am Pistis."

Perhaps this first introduction does not make much sense to you right now—but please bear with me. I will share how I came to discover this part of myself and why I choose to embrace it as part of my identity.

I am not the first person to describe themselves this way, and I certainly will not be the last. What amazes me is that this realization came to me *before* I had ever read any spiritual books or listened to spiritual teachers.

Later, I discovered that teachers like Neville Goddard and Bob Proctor—both known for their teachings on consciousness and divine creation—had long taught about the identity I had felt within me.

So how did I come to understand the same truths they taught, without studying their work before? That is when I understood that *Divine knowledge is real,* and that the unseen first made itself known to me long before I had words for prejudice or resilience...

I was born and raised in a Christian family, so any knowledge outside of my Christian faith was never really of interest for me. I was taught to be obedient, but my family was also open to me exploring my own truth—as long as it remained within the framework of Christianity.

Because within Christianity, there are many

layers—such as Catholicism, Protestantism, non-denominational churches, and more; I was always free to explore different perspectives, as long as they pointed toward Christ. However, the exploration of other religions or belief systems was never part of the conversation. It was not that it was forbidden—it simply never came up.

While the world gave me labels—Woman, Christian, Black, immigrant—something deeper within me kept nudging me to look beyond them, to question whether I was more than what I had been told I was. That deeper knowing started speaking to me very early on...

I must have been about five or six years old when I had a first experience that my entire family can testify to—an experience that revealed just how attuned I was to my inner voice...

Psychologists might call it intuition, theologians, the whisper of the Holy Spirit. Or you might call it *"the voice of an angel," "inner guidance," "spirit,"* or *"consciousness."* Whatever the name we give it, I have come to understand that it serves the same purpose: to protect us and direct us to our authentic self.

It was an afternoon, maybe around 4 or 5 p.m. I was playing in the front yard at my grandmother's house, where our family was living at the time. I was outside, playing alone, near the hibiscus flowers.

Our house had a front gate, and in the front yard, there were little spots where my family planted flowers and garden herbs. I especially loved playing near the hibiscus bushes. The flowers had a sweet liquid that I liked to taste, and I often tucked them into my hair because they were so beautiful.

The late-afternoon light in my old neighborhood turned everything a low amber—dust motes drifting like tiny suns above the cracked cement. The hibiscus petals stained my fingertips red; even now, when I smell their faint, tangy sweetness, I am back in that yard, small and barefoot, listening to a world no one else seemed to hear.

I was perfectly content in those hours, happily lost inside a kingdom no one else could see—arranging my dolls beneath the shade of the hibiscus bushes, threading the petals into tiny crowns, and letting the blossoms' scent become the perfume of an imagined court. The outside world dissolved; all that mattered was the soft murmur of leaves, the sun-warm earth against my knees, and the secret conversations I staged between dolls and flowers. Within that small, blooming universe, I needed nothing more.

Suddenly, I began to hear an inner voice speaking to me. It was not my own, but it sounded like an adult's voice.

"Sam." It whispered.

The name sounded through my mind like a soft bell. I froze mid-game. My dolls were still balanced on a twig-ladder of hibiscus stems. I looked around the yard. No one. Only the hush of late-afternoon heat.

"Sam, listen."

The voice was inside my head. Unmistakably adult—low, steady, and unmistakably feminine. It carried the calm authority of a teacher.

"I need you to go to your parents' bedroom, climb onto the bed, and push back the loose square in the ceiling."

The Whisper That Knew Me

I swallowed hard, doll forgotten.

"Why?" I whispered to no one.

"There is a toy hidden up there," she said. "You have to go now. It is right above your parents' bed—hidden by the ceiling."

The certainty in her tone unsettled me more than her request. One moment I was stitching leaf-capes for my queens; the next, a grown woman's voice was mapping secret treasure in the ceiling. I sat very still, trying to decide whether I was up to this adventure.

"You have to go now," it insisted.

I looked around the yard. I did not see my parents, though they may have been nearby. The house felt quieter than usual—eerily calm. No brothers running through the rooms. No aunts chatting over food. Just stillness.

I remember thinking, *really? A toy? In the ceiling?* It seemed odd—even impossible—but the voice was so persistent, so urgent, that I did not question too much. I walked inside.

It guided me step by step:

"Take the chairs from the dining table. Stack them. Climb onto the bed. Push open the ceiling."

And I listened.

I did not feel afraid, but only excited. I dragged the dining chairs, one by one, into my parents' room. No one stopped me. No one was there. The house remained silent as if time itself had paused for me.

The voice felt so real that I started talking back out loud: "How should I move the chairs? I'm not sure I can reach." I said.

Step by step, I was coached to where to place my foot and how to steady my hand. When I reached the bed, I climbed up carefully, following every instruction, until the ceiling panel was within reach and my fear was replaced by the strange certainty that I was about to discover whatever waited above.

I had never looked up at the ceiling that way before—not that close. It was made of thick cardboard, not the kind I would imagine being removable. But the voice kept urging:

"You can do it. There is something for you to find."

I noticed a small opening in the ceiling. The voice said again: "Yes. That is the place. Open it."

I pushed it open, and it was darker up there than I expected. First, my fingers brushed against something. I hesitated for a moment. My heart thudded—not from fear, but from anticipation. I wanted to reach it. I wanted to see.

This time, I was on tiptoe, forgetting entirely that I was standing on a chair atop the bed. I reached further and saw a box—but no toy.

I remember feeling disappointed. *There is nothing here*, I thought. But the voice interrupted firmly: "Yes—that is the box. Grab it. Take it. Now."

I pushed myself farther, reached for the box, and the moment I grabbed it, everything moved fast. Too fast for memory to fully catch. Part of the ceiling collapsed with me. The chairs wobbled, and in one sudden motion, I was falling.

I fell but landed safely on the bed—as if I had just jumped. The box and chairs hit the floor, and the sound echoed through the house.

My parents and other family members rushed into the room. But instead of being upset about the mess, they were visibly shocked by what had been found in the box. Their concern shifted quickly from the ceiling to the box's contents. They asked if I was okay—and I was completely fine. They asked me what made me go up there—a question

The Whisper That Knew Me

with no logical answer.

I simply told them the truth: "A voice in my head told me there was a toy hidden in the ceiling. She told me how to get it, and I listened."

I remember explaining, with the innocence of a child, how I had been calmly playing outside when the voice told me to go to my parents' bedroom and to reach the ceiling. I described how the voice walked me through each step—how I knew exactly where to go and what to do. I had been taught to always tell the truth, even if it sounded absurd—and I did.

My parents believed me. They did not scold me or even mention the mess. They were somehow... relieved. Grateful, even. Because what I found was a toy—but at least not for me.

Later, I came to understand that the box contained a kind of strange magical compilation—a sort of witchcraft setup with dolls, and what looked like a miniature coffin. Other items surrounded them; all seemingly arranged with dark intent.

The voice did not lie to me. There *was* something there. There *was* a "toy." Just not one meant for me.

Could someone really harm my family by hiding a spiritual weapon in our ceiling? I still do not have the answer. But what I know is that I had been guided to remove it.

For a long time, I did not think about the event. I was a child. I often played alone with my dolls, and it always felt like I was talking to someone—or someone was talking to me. Only years later did I realize the meaning of that moment. And, as more experiences unfolded throughout my life, I came to the clear and unwavering realization that *I am guided*. I fully accept it.

I have come to understand that I am not just a

body, a name, or a role. I am also spiritual. As such, I am a spirit—eternally connected, divinely guided. And I believe, perhaps... *you are too.*

So now, let me truly ask you: have you ever thought of who you might be beyond your name, title or background? Has there ever been a moment when your inner voice whispered to you?

Pause for a moment and move through your own memory. Remember the instant you felt an unexplained pull to call someone, turn left instead of right, or speak a truth you did not plan to confess. Recall the warm flood of peace that followed—or the restless itch that came when you ignored it.

For a long time now, my own whisper has said, *we are more than we appear. We are loved. We are guided. We are divine.* If that is true—if something wiser is always reaching for us—then our work is simple, though not always easy: to remember, to open the heart, and to listen on purpose.

As you move into the pages ahead, treat every story and practice as a reflection. Hold it up to your ordinary moments, watch what glimmers, and let those glimmers lead you back to the place where the quiet voice has been waiting all along.

CHAPTER 2

TRUSTING THE UNSEEN IS TRUSTING YOURSELF

It was around 8:15 on a Monday morning, and I was on my way to work. I put on my morning Amazon Music playlist, preparing myself for a good day. Well—it was Monday, so there was nothing particularly exciting about it, I thought. It was just the typical 9-to-5 routine I had agreed upon with my employer. I took I-4 every day because it was the quickest route to my destination.

I had become accustomed to the idea that part of my morning would always be a mix of braking, crawling through traffic, and speeding up whenever I could to avoid additional delays. There were usually 17 minutes where I had to be fully focused on the road—where nothing and no one could distract me. I often drove in the left lane, as it was usually the fastest.

While driving, fully focused, I suddenly received a strange inner instruction to move to the lane next to me.

"Move to the middle lane." I heard.

"Why?" I asked inwardly. "There is absolutely no reason to change lanes now. There is hardly any traffic in mine..."

I do not know why it felt important to argue or

search for an explanation. Maybe it was because I was certain *I was right*—there was no logical reason to change lanes. But still, it insisted:

"Move now."

I hesitated for a second, then checked my mirrors, and changed lanes. As soon as I did, a car came barreling out of the express lane, cutting violently into the left lane—right where I had just been. It was so sudden, I flinched. The car swerved past me and kept going, nearly losing control.

I blinked. I shook my head, realizing just how close I had come to an accident on I-4.

"Thank you." I said out loud to the voice that guided me.

So, what was this "voice" that guided me? What is the "unseen"? Why trust it? Why even talk about it?

This also reminded me that, one night, I was in the car with someone I was dating. He was driving in the left lane when he suddenly shifted all the way to the right.

"Why did you change lanes?" I asked.

"I don't know," he replied. "I just *felt* like I needed to slow down."

A few minutes later, we noticed that two police cars had pulled over the vehicles we had been following in the left lane. Then, more unmarked police cars appeared along the highway.

"Unbelievable," he said, turning to me, "I was that close to getting a ticket tonight!"

That moment showed me that the inner voice, the unseen guidance, the quiet feeling that I am talking about, is not just for me. It comes to all of us, and more often than we realize.

✦ ✦ ✦

Trusting the Unseen Is Trusting Yourself

Across cultures and spiritual traditions, the unseen is known by many names—spirit, intuition, divine presence, the higher self, the soul, or simply mystery. When I feel a pull toward something I had not consciously thought of, I have learned now to pay attention; because to me, the unseen is not an invisible creature following us around or trying to interfere in our lives, but it is *us*—a part of ourselves we cannot always perceive, yet more aware and actively searching for a relationship with the physical self.

The more the unseen tried to communicate with me, the more I began noticing patterns—especially the difference between when I listened and when I did not. Eventually, I came to realize that trusting the unseen—that voice within—is trusting myself.

Some of the teachings I had learned in the past about the Divine and how it communicates began to feel lighter. The more I was experiencing guidance, the more I found myself seeking a deeper understanding, wondering how many others have experienced this relationship between their physical self and their invisible self.

Then, I realized that there comes a moment in every spiritual journey when one stops asking others for permission to be whole and starts listening inward. This is where everything begins.

I began to understand that some wisdom is carried within—not even learned but somehow remembered. Sometimes, information is received through intuition, dreams, or inner knowing. They just did not come from a book or a mentor.

As I questioned the clarity of my understanding of myself and of life, I realized that some parts of my spiritual journey also begin through disruption. It came as an internal battle between what is logical, what has been taught, and what is being experienced.

Somehow, something unexplainable stirred within me. Sometimes it was restlessness; other time it was the ache that whispers: *"There must be more."* I began to sense that the life I built on a surface level no longer holds *my* truth. I started searching—not only for answers, but for alignment.

At first, it felt like a rebellion. A discomfort. I began to question things I was taught to never doubt. Are we truly alone? Are we only flesh, blood and brain? Is there more? If yes, what?

After spending time questioning, mapping, and exploring the symbolism of my life, I came to the realization of making my *sacred return to self.* The sacred return to self is my way of choosing to become more than who I was told to be. It was a return to who I have always been beneath the noise.

It was not a loud arrival. It was an unfolding. Like remembering a song I once knew by heart. Somehow, something ancient awakens inside me and began to lead me—not forward, but inward.

I came to understand that I could read countless books and follow many spiritual teachers, but the voice I was truly listening to came from within. Whether I accepted it, understood it, or not, it was a part of me. A part of my awareness, my consciousness, and my being. And so, I realized that the greatest step was to *trust* the unseen, and in doing so, to trust *myself.*

Many of us say the strongest relationships are built on trust. So, if you feel at ease when someone shows you qualities that earn your trust, then how confident are you in trusting yourself? When your inner voice whispers, "Go left," but you choose to go right, why is there something that makes you doubt? Do you believe that your own voice could misguide you?

Just as I had to make the sacred return to self to learn how and when my voice speaks, I now understand that before you can fully trust yourself, you must first *meet* yourself—truly, gently, and deeply. Because if you have never taken the time to encounter your true self, how will you know when it speaks? How will you recognize its sound? And how will you ever learn to trust it?

Many people, including earlier versions of myself, move through life without ever forming a partnership of trust with themselves. Without that inner alliance, choices become dictated by external expectations, and the wisdom within is drowned out by the noise of the world.

Therefore, that is precisely where the journey begins: Not with definitions, achievements, or expectations—but, with quiet awareness and self-discovery.

The moment you begin asking: *"Who am I, beyond all this?"*—that is the beginning of spiritual awakening.

✦ ✦ ✦

In many ancient traditions, there is knowledge of this same sacred return. One of the most poetic comes from the Tao Te Ching, a foundational text of Chinese philosophy written by Lao Tzu.

The Tao speaks not of doctrines, but of the *Way*—the natural, flowing intelligence that moves through all life. It reminds us that to access what is eternal, we must surrender to what is unseen.

> *"Can the mystic gate to all life essence be opened or closed without the virtue of the mysterious nature?"*

PISTIS: The Art of Trusting the Unseen

—Tao Te Ching, Chapter 10

Here, the Tao reminds us that access to the deepest truths—and therefore, to ourselves—requires a relationship with mystery.

When I speak of mystery, I am not referring to something dark or unreachable. I mean the unseen flow that moves through all things. The inner guidance that cannot always be explained, the synchronicities that arrive without warning, the quiet knowing that defies logic. To have a relationship with mystery means to walk through life with reverence for what you do not yet understand. It means learning to trust what you *feel* before you can explain it. It is not about having the answer; it is about staying open, present, and humble enough to receive them when they come.

Therefore, the relationship with mystery is not something we force or conquer, but something we learn to move with.

To walk the path of trust, it becomes important to learn how to flow with what arrives in our life and to be receptive to its hidden teachings. The *mystic gate to all life essence* cannot be opened if we ignore the subtle language of our surroundings, and if we fail to recognize when life itself is speaking to us. This is why the Tao emphasizes the *"virtue of the mysterious nature."*

Everything around us—and within us—is dressed in mystery. The gate of the sacred return to self is unlocked through our ability to become mystery ourselves.

Let me take this thought even further.

I believe that many of the problems we are facing today; like some forms of anxiety, uncertainty and fear—do not just come from our circumstances. They come from not knowing who we are.

Just as it takes getting to know others before we can trust them, the same is true for ourselves—if we do not know who we are, we cannot truly trust ourselves.

Now, who we are—that depends on us. Do you believe you are here simply to live and survive? Do you think you are defined by your title, your job, or your role within your family? Do you believe you are divine? Just human? Or have you simply never had the chance to stop and ask yourself: *Who am I, really?*

My sacred return has taught me that trusting the unseen is not blind faith. It is a deep partnership and understanding of who I am. It is a conscious recognition of my own divine origin. It was not a fanatical belief rooted in religion or what I was taught to accept, but an inner knowing born from the unfolding and transformation within me. It requires that I *choose* and *know* that something greater is guiding me, something greater lives in me, and therefore, something greater *is* me.

Let me give you an example:

Imagine—just imagine—the greatest, richest, most powerful, and wisest man you have ever heard of. If no one comes to mind, simply imagine that he exists.

Now picture this:

One day, someone knocks at your door and says:

"I am a messenger from the palace of the greatest, richest, most powerful, and wisest man on earth. We have been watching over you since the day you were born, because this man is your biological father. And now, he wants you to know the truth, so you can step into your inheritance. He wants you to know who you are."

Naturally, you would be in shock.
"How is this possible?"
"Can I trust this?"
"What do they want from me?"
"Is this some kind of mistake?"

You might be skeptical. You might be excited. You might even reject it entirely. But none of that changes the fact that—this is who you are. Whether you accept it or not, whether you choose to claim your inheritance or walk away from it—your origin remains the same.

Now, apply this to your spiritual self: imagine that you are part of a family far greater than what you can perceive—that you are connected to invisible parts of yourself, to something far more expansive than you have ever imagined, and that your inheritance is already written within you.

The question is not simply, *"Is it true?"* but rather, *"Am I ready to accept who I am?"*

Earlier, I said: *"In order to trust yourself, you have to meet yourself first."* This is the moment when all the external noise fades—and you finally *see* yourself. Will you accept what you see? Will you trust the voice that is guiding you? Will you trust *yourself*?

✦ ✦ ✦

Loving yourself is also part of your trust.
Many people talk about the importance of *"loving ourselves."* But how can you genuinely love someone you have never met?

True self-love begins only after you meet your authentic Self, and you learn to build trust and partnership with it.

In Christianity, this is sometimes called being *born again*. It refers to a *spiritual rebirth*, which is a transformation of the inner self that occurs when a person accepts their divine relationship and commits to a life of faith. In other word, it is the "death" of the old self to embrace the divine self.

In many other spiritual paths, it is also known as *initiation*. It is a sacred rite of passage marking the beginning of a deeper level of spiritual awareness, responsibility, or belonging. Unlike simply learning information, initiation involves an inner transformation and also a symbolic "death" of the old self and awakening into a new spiritual identity.

Spirituality itself is the personal and often transformative journey of seeking connection—within oneself, with others, with nature, and with something greater than the visible world. It is not limited to religious practices or doctrines, though it may include them. At its core, spirituality is about asking deeper questions: *What makes me? Why am I here? What connects me to life, love, and meaning?* It is the inner path that guides us toward truth, balance, and purpose. Whether experienced through silence, prayer, intuition, awe, or love, spirituality invites us to listen more closely to the unseen, to trust what we feel deeply, and to live in alignment with our highest self.

Therefore, whatever name you choose to call this spiritual turning point—whether *born again* or *initiation*—it all begins with receiving a *Divine Invitation.*

One day, you will feel an energetic pull—an inner prompting that urges you to act. I call it a *"Divine Invitation."*

It may not be a call to attend church, and not necessarily for you to follow a particular teacher or preacher. But it will be an invitation to *become yourself*—to finally *meet* yourself. Not as others told you to be; not as the world expects you to perform, but as who you *truly* are. You will feel called to do something that only you can see—to trust a project that only you can birth, or to speak your truth in a way that only you can voice.

Whether you know it or not, this will be your initiation—the symbolic death of the old version of yourself to embrace who you truly are. And it will begin with a choice: To accept the invitation to listen to what you cannot see and trust yourself—or to step back.

If you choose to listen and act in faith—even without all the answers, even without the visible tools to make it happen—but you move forward anyway, because deep inside, *you know that you know* the best will happen, without explanation or proof; then, congratulations—you have accepted the invitation.

You have accepted this first step that has helped you to break into the unseen.

You have come to understand—consciously or unconsciously—that you can listen and trust the voice within and therefore have the keys that open doors to many possibilities. You will start seeing yourself in clear visions; and right after that moment, your spiritual transformation begins...

Just as any relationship built on trust will face moments that test it, you too will be called to discover how deeply you can trust yourself and the voice guiding you toward your truest self; and, for that to happen you will enter the life of a butterfly.

First from caterpillar, you will pass through your cocoon: a quiet, lonely, transformative phase. There, you will begin to learn more about yourself like never before.

In the natural world, the caterpillar's transformation is known as complete metamorphosis. It passes through four stages: egg,

Trusting the Unseen Is Trusting Yourself

larva, pupa, and adult. But it is in the pupa, in the stillness of the cocoon, that true transformations happen.

The caterpillar does not grow wings while crawling. It must first enter a pause. A chrysalis, where everything it once was, begins to dissolve.

Inside the cocoon, the caterpillar disintegrates. Its old form melts into a formless state. Cells break down. Patterns dissolve. There is no structure left to cling to, no certainty to hold onto. What once crawled no longer exists.

This is not a soft becoming. It is an unraveling.

There is no map. No promise that anything beautiful will emerge. Just darkness. Stillness, like a suspension...

And yet—it is within this undoing that something greater begins to stir.

You will come to understand that it was never the teachings, the friendships, or the sense of safety that made you whole; it was something far deeper—something you carried within you all along. You will start creating a bond with yourself that no fear can break.

You will meet a version of you that you are no longer afraid to love, to speak of, or to empower. The version of you that knows is guided by something greater than itself.

Then, you will feel a sense of purpose. A purpose that is aligned with who you have been for a very long time. A purpose that does not arise from ego, but from a deep sense of belonging. This is where your love for yourself and your trust begin.

✦ ✦ ✦

In any spiritual path—transformation or the

rebirth of the self—often does not come to comfort you; it comes to awaken you. It strips you of everything that was built on fear, survival, and illusion. It calls you to release identities that once felt necessary but no longer fit the shape of your soul.

For it to move in that way, it must arise from a natural flow—a genuine invitation—not something fleeting or externally influenced. And once this transformation takes place, you will be changed forever. The cocoon will break, and the butterfly will emerge—beautiful, confident and free to explore paths that were never possible as a caterpillar.

You will step into your own world of possibilities, because you will come to *understand* that something greater lives in you.

Now, you might ask me: Why does it require such a dramatic transformation just to know ourselves? Can we just not awaken one day, already flying? Is it not possible to be born an eagle—already soaring? And to that, I will say: all birds, even the majestic ones, must first learn how to fly.

The Divine Invitation is the doorway you open within yourself that, once entered, can never be closed. Because now—you truly *know*. You have tasted the truth in the depths of your soul. You have touched waters so deep that no storm, no wave, no fear can drown you.

You have met a version of yourself that is no longer waiting to be discovered in someone else's mirror. A version that is no longer shaped by approval or imitation. Your sacred self is no longer a duplication—it is the *original* of an expression of something that only you can carry.

It requires a transformation because it demands something from you: *A willingness* to let go.

Trusting the Unseen Is Trusting Yourself

A trust that even in the melting, you are becoming. *A knowing*, that once you have emerged, you will never again doubt your wings.

Have you ever paused to wonder where in your life you have resisted the cocoon, and what might have emerged if, instead of fighting it, you had *trust yourself...?*

You may not describe the deep changes in your life using these words. You may not even consider yourself spiritual or fully understand what is unfolding—and that is perfectly okay. The Divine Invitation is for everyone. These are the moments of transformation that call us to act not only from what we know, but from something deeper within us. And once you accept that invitation—whether consciously or unconsciously—your life will not remain the same. Because that is the moment you begin stepping into your highest, truest self.

This step in your life will not happen by chance. It will happen because you choose to listen to a silent voice and trust the visions of your becoming.

Let me give you one more example:

Imagine a well-known public figure is refused entry into a restaurant—not because of who she is, but because the concierge did not recognize her. What is the first question someone might ask that employee?

"How could you not recognize this person?"

"Don't you know who this is?"

And once the truth is revealed, everything changes.

The atmosphere shifts.

The respect returns.

The attitude transforms.

This story may be fictional, but reflect on it for a moment. Think about the well-known people you know and the VIP treatment they receive—simply because of *who they are.*

Now, let me ask you this:

When fear rises...

When your circumstances try to limit you...

When doubt knocks on your door...

Would you not want to look at those things and say: *"Don't you know who I am?"*

But here is the key—you can only say that if you truly *know* yourself. Not just *believe* it. Because *belief* still carries the shadow of doubt. As in *"I believe* I have a purple dress," is different than *"I know* I have a purple dress."

✦ ✦ ✦

If the unseen knocks at your door—offering a Divine Invitation to meet your true Self—and you choose, out of fear, doubt, or disbelief, to ignore it or turn away, life often responds with what I call "lessons."

I believe we are here to learn, and whether we realize it or not—consciously or unconsciously—we are also here to meet ourselves. Lessons, then, are not punishments or mere hardships. They are recurring experiences that emerge exactly where our trust is fragile, our vision unclear, or our connection to the deeper Self still uncertain. Each moment serves as a mirror, reflecting the parts of our inner landscape that are still longing for healing, clarity, and alignment with our true rhythm.

Sometimes, we begin to notice the same themes reappearing in our lives: a relationship that tests our boundaries; a situation that evokes deep fear or insecurity; or a moment that demands we choose between old conditioning and our inner voice. These patterns are not coincidences—they are our *lessons*. But to truly understand them, we must become aware, present, and willing to ask questions that connect us to ourselves: *Do I see it this time? Do I trust what I feel? Why can't I trust my own voice? Etc.*

Lessons are how our inner compass guide us back to ourselves. Not to the self that others told us to be—but the self that knows.

So, if you ever wonder why certain patterns keep returning to your life; take it as your invitation to ask what is this trying to teach you about *inner trust*.

Remember that free will is the gate between fear and faith. The Divine will never force you—it will only invite you.

> *"There are natural transformation processes which simply happen to us, whether we like it or not, and whether we know it or not. These processes develop considerable psychic effects, which would be sufficient in themselves to make any thoughtful person ask himself what really happened to him."*
> —Carl Jung (The Collected works of C.G. Jung, Vol9)

Life's unfolding will, sooner or later, return you to your own doorway. Whether you understand it or want it or not—meeting yourself is part of your discovery, as you cannot reclaim your power until you know who you are. And in this quest of knowing who you are, you inevitably begin to wonder where you come from and what breathes life into that sacred memory...

✦ ✦ ✦

The unseen is "unseen" because it cannot be seen. Therefore, we call it *"unseen."* But how can we truly name something we cannot perceive with our eyes? Perhaps it is because we can *feel* it.

Often, our desire to name the unseen arises because something has been *felt* before it was ever *understood*.

In the same way, when we *"feel something"*—an inner prompting, a presence, or a sense of guidance—we instinctively want to name the unseen. Naturally, we seek to know more about ourselves, our world, and the forces that shape us. Just like the air we breathe, the pull of gravity, or the warmth of love resting on our chest, we have named these unseen forces that cannot be perceived with the naked eye—yet shape our lives every single day.

Have you ever thought about what you truly mean when you say you love someone? What is it that you are trying to share with that person? Is it not an unseen force—something within, something deeply felt, yet invisible? You see, when you look closely, the unseen is not as inaccessible as you might think. It breathes with you.

For a long time, people died from carbon monoxide poisoning without understanding that an invisible danger could even exist. It took science, awareness, and openness to recognize what the eyes alone could not. And today, countless particles once thought invisible or unimaginable are being studied, named, and measured—simply because we dared to believe there was more.

So, what if we allowed ourselves to be that open to the possibility that our eyes, ears, nose, tongue, and fingertips are *not* the only ways we perceive truth? What if those senses are just one layer of a much greater knowing waiting to be awakened?

We are often told that we only have five senses: sight, hearing, touch, taste, and smell. But in truth,

Trusting the Unseen Is Trusting Yourself

we are equipped with much more. There are senses science now recognizes that go beyond the physical—like balance, internal awareness, pain, temperature, and even the perception of time. And still, I believe there are others that language and measurement have yet to fully name—like the sense of spiritual alignment, intuitive knowing, or feeling the energy in a room before a word is spoken. So, when I invite you to trust in the unseen, I am not asking you to abandon your senses. I am asking you to *expand* them.

The sacred return to self to trust the unseen requires more than physical awareness. It requires a union with all aspects of perceptions, because some truths do not speak to the body alone, they also speak within. They communicate in forms we cannot yet fully perceive or understand.

Think about it: your phone, your microwave, your GPS—all depend on invisible forces. Have you ever wondered why we, as humans, are able to create technologies that function through unseen systems? Perhaps it is because the inspiration for these inventions is already part of life itself. You cannot see Wi-Fi waves—but they are there, carrying your voice, your messages, your presence across the world in seconds.

There was a time—not long ago—when the idea of the internet seemed impossible. People laughed at the thought that one day, we could communicate across continents without wires, without letters, without even speaking. The idea that invisible waves could carry entire conversations, videos, emotions, and real-time presence felt like science fiction. And yet—here we are. What once sounded irrational is now how we live, connect, and exist each day.

So, if we can build machines that transmit

energy and intelligence through the unseen, is it really so strange to imagine that the universe itself operates on a similar, but even grander scale? Maybe we are not inventing the unseen—we are simply *mirroring* what has always existed.

> *"Nature has its way to be more creative than we are. So, we have always been surprised by what we can see in the sky."*
> — Dr. John C. Mather (Senior Project Scientist on James Webb Space Telescope (JWST)

To truly understand that there are unseen forces—including invisible parts of ourselves—means recognizing that life is more than what we can touch, measure, or logically explain. Therefore, trusting and communicating with the unseen is to know that we are not alone in our journey—not even within ourselves.

Now, if—like me—you know that something greater is at work, then you may begin to see that just as invisible technologies shape your daily life, unseen forces are also at play, moving energy and order across this planet. These are forces you can sense, feel, hear, and begin to understand. And with time, you may come to recognize that something even greater—something that does not need a name—is the Source of all alignment, order, and consciousness.

Once you begin to trust your inner guidance, once you fully return to yourself, you will realize that you do not need a screen or a device to connect to that Source. The unseen part of you—the part you have learned to meet, to trust, and to cherish—is already wired to it. And when you listen closely, you will hear it speaking through many voices, yet always as One Source.

CHAPTER 3

THE SOURCE OF MANY VOICES, BUT ONE ORIGIN

There is a Sacred Intelligence that cannot be named. It has been translated into a thousand languages. It has been worshipped through fire, song, silence, water and breath. It has been painted in temples and whispered in forests.

Some call it God. Others call it the Universe, Spirit, The All, The I AM, Brahman, Shiva, Oshun, Atum, BonDye, The Tao, The Great Spirit, The Great Mother or simply Love—yet no name can fully contain it.

Across time, centuries, and civilizations, humanity has shared one enduring pursuit: the search for the Divine. From the earliest cave paintings to the construction of temples, from prayers to rituals to trance, people across every culture and continent have longed to understand something greater than themselves. This yearning reflects the desire to connect with the unseen, the eternal and the sacred, as a deep and timeless part of our human nature.

The search for a mystical connection is something I could not truly understand without first experiencing the need to understand myself. Often, we are born into families that guide us toward a specific belief system. Whether we realize it or not, we are shaped by the teachings passed down to us. Some of us are never encouraged to look beyond those boundaries. Some of us feel too confident in our own version of the truth. Others are simply afraid to question, fearing it might be considered a sin, and that they could somehow be punished just for thinking differently. As if, in matters of spirit, it exists a kind of silent dictatorship that forbids us from seeking deeper guidance.

I remember a time when I, too, could not understand how the Divine could be called by different names. That was because I was often taught to focus on the *image* assigned to it, rather than the *energy* behind the names. And when I was only seeing the form and not the essence, it became harder for me to recognize that many names may, in truth, be pointing to the same sacred energy.

Now, I know that these names are not competing truths—they are reflections of the same Source, seen through different eyes. The Divine, in its wisdom, speaks to every heart in the language it can understand. That is why I believe that no one path holds the full picture. And yet—each is sacred, because it reflects the desire to return, and therefore to truly know ourselves.

> *"All day I think about it, then at night I say it. Where did I come from, and what am I supposed to be doing? I have no idea. My soul is from elsewhere, I am sure of that, and I intend to end up there [...] whoever brought me here will have to take me home."*
> —Rumi (The Essential Rumi)

"Are we spiritually orphaned?" I asked myself one day.

"Why do you ask?" My inner voice responded.

"The longing for "home"—by whatever name

we give it (paradise, heaven, nirvana, and so on)—felt to me like a sign of spiritual trauma, like children waiting for parents who never return. Or like children who have lost their way home, unsure of which direction to take to find it again. Somehow, they wait with hope that one day they will be reunited—and that, in that moment, all inner pain will finally disappear. Otherwise, why are we even waiting? What is it, really, that we are waiting for?" I said.

I was filled with questions. Not so much about the Divine itself—I have always sensed its presence in the natural order of the sun, the moon, the water, and the seasons. That alone is evidence of higher power. But I began to question the instructions we are often given: to wait, to ask, to *pray*—instead of to connect, to embrace and to *know* our divine nature.

Etymologically, the word *pray* comes from the Latin *precari*, meaning "to beg" or "to entreat." Therefore, are we somehow outside of that sacred order, waiting to be seen and chosen? Or are we already part of it—an extension of it—forgotten only by our own disconnection? I wanted to know...

To explain the Divine, most sacred texts begin their revelations by describing the creation of our world. They speak of land, light, animals, oceans, and the arrival of humankind. But very few go into detail about the creation of the entire universe. Why? Perhaps because, even in their sacred beauty, these writings reflect the level of awareness humanity could hold at the time they were received.

Our spiritual senses are often limited to what we

can see, name, or explain. And while I believe that the Source is infinite, I also know that our perception of it evolves over time. As we awaken and explore more deeply—both within and beyond—we begin to access truths that earlier generations could only sense in part. This is why newer spiritual texts and revelations inspired by ancient texts, often explore themes of vibration, consciousness, multidimensionality, or cosmic origin—because humanity is now slowly ready to receive them.

Let's take the Book of Genesis in the Bible, Chapter 2, as an example. There are verses that stand quietly, often overlooked, but filled with mystery:

> "*5 And every plant of the field before it was in the earth, and every herb of the field before it grew: for the Lord God had not caused it to rain upon the earth, and there was not a man to till the ground.*
> *6 **But** there went up a mist from the earth, and watered the whole face of the ground.*
> *7 **And** the Lord God formed man of the dust of the ground, and breathed into his nostrils the breath of life; and man became a living soul.*"
> —Genesis 2:5-7 (KJV)

Some spiritual teachers who study Genesis can offer a unique perspective: that before any divine command to shape man from dust, before any declaration of dominion, there was something else—a mist. A rising force of water. A movement independent of instruction. It is this mist that makes the soil fertile. A quiet element that gave life the condition to emerge. No spoken word caused it to rise—it simply did.

Others may come with different explanations,

The Source of Many Voices, but One Origin

grounded in the belief that all things were created by divine command. And that is also worthy of respect.

Whatever your position may be, I believe this passage reveals something deeper: some aspects of creation exist as part of a greater rhythm. Whether or not there were instructions, life began because water moved.

I believe this because spiritually and scientifically, water is what shapes and sustains life here. Oceans cover more than 70% of the planet. Every cell of our body holds water. Life came not from dry land, but from the depths of movement, fluidity and flow. Humans are formed in water in their mother's wombs—and naturally, the water broke to open to life.

And yet, we named this planet "Earth."

We passively accepted this name, even though we know about the importance of water.

> *"Earth – our home planet – is the third planet from the Sun, and the fifth largest planet."*
> —science.nasa.gov (About the Planets)

Logic might argue we should have called the planet Water. But we did not. And that, too, is acceptable—because language is often shaped by what we choose to see, and what we are taught to value. And sometimes, the deepest truths are the ones we overlook.

This is a simple example of how our understanding, while sincere, is often partial. And the more we open ourselves to explore beyond what we are taught, the more clarity and spiritual remembrance we can receive. And the same is true for every belief system.

Each faith tradition, each path, each sacred story

holds fragments of truth.

I believe that the Source is so vast, that its truth has reached humanity in countless forms: through sacred texts, rituals, songs, science, visions and dreams. Through Christianity, Islam, Judaism, Hinduism, Buddhism, including Indigenous, African, Asian, Caribbean, and other ancestral traditions whose wisdom was passed orally or ritually rather than written. None are wrong and none contain the whole. Each offers a glimpse of the Infinite, filtered through time, language, and level of understanding of those it touched.

Just as the warmth of the sun is not felt the same way everywhere on Earth, the way we experience the Divine is also not the same. Scientifically, the Earth is tilted on its axis at about 23.5 degrees, which means different regions receive varying amounts of sunlight depending on the time of year and their position on the globe. Near the equator, sunlight hits more directly, making it feel hotter and more intense. Farther from the equator or during winter months, the sun's rays arrive at a lower angle and pass through more of the atmosphere, making the warmth less concentrated. Altitude also plays a role—higher elevations receive stronger sunlight because there is less atmosphere to filter it. All of these factors mean that while the sun is always shining, how we feel its warmth depends on where we are and the conditions around us.

In the same way, the Divine is always present, but how we experience it, depends on our position in life, our openness, our inner climate. Just as no one location can claim the sun shines only for them, no one path or person can truly define how the Divine appears. The difference is not in the presence of light or love, but in how each of us is

The Source of Many Voices, but One Origin

positioned to perceive and receive it.

Because our languages are also different, the same sun is pronounced in many ways—*sol, sun, soleil, shams, helios, etc.*—yet no matter how it is spoken, it refers to the same celestial body, shining over all of us without distinction. This simple realization reveals that diversity in expression does not negate unity in essence. Just as cultures across the globe name the sun differently while pointing to the same source of light, so too do spiritual paths to describe the Divine using different names, symbols, and languages.

Whether one says God, Source, Universe, Allah, Yahweh, Brahman, Tao, BonDye, and so on—the essence being described is not many, but *One*. The difference lies not in the truth itself, but in the lens through which each people has come to know it. Just as the sun rises for all, the Divine reaches all—regardless of the name we use to speak of it.

Therefore, I come to realize that religions are not rival maps—they are regional dialects trying to describe the same sky. Yes, some teachings have been misunderstood. Yes, some have been twisted to serve power, to instill fear and to create unspoken rules of *morality*. But the light behind them—the Source that first inspired them—is often never lost. It remains available, waiting to be *felt* beneath the surface.

For so long, I was taught that truth belongs to a single path—that only one tradition holds the fullness of the Divine. But as I am connecting to the unseen, I begin to sense something different: a truth that cannot be confined to one book, one group of people, or one belief. I begin to understand that the Divine speaks in many voices—and that the thread of love, wisdom, and remembrance weaves through them all.

PISTIS: The Art of Trusting the Unseen

✦ ✦ ✦

Long before modern religions began shaping our understanding of the Creator, the people of ancient Kemet—what we now call Egypt—left behind sacred writings that reached for the mystery of divine origin. *The Pyramid Texts*, inscribed over 4,300 years ago, are the oldest known religious texts in human history. In them, the Creator is called Atum—a self-begotten force who rose alone from the formless waters of Nun to birth all that exists.

Atum was not imagined as separate from creation, but as its very essence—forming the world not through domination, but through divine emergence.

In Kemet, the Divine was not locked into one form. Atum, Ptah, Ra, and Amun were seen not as separate gods, but as expressions reflecting a different aspect of the Infinite.

Ptah, for instance, was said to have created all things through thought and speech—mirroring the principle that the universe is mental, spiritual, and vibrational at its core.

> *"There came into being as the heart and there came into being as the tongue [something] in the form of Atum. The mighty Great One is Ptah, who transmitted [life to all gods], as well as to their ka's, through this heart, by which Horus had become Ptah, and through this tongue, by which Thoth became Ptah."*
> —Memphite Theology.

Like Kemet's Ptah or Genesis and the Gospel of John's "Word;"

The Source of Many Voices, but One Origin

"In the beginning was the Word, and the Word was with God, and the Word was God."
—John 1:1 (NIV)

Hinduism also teaches that the universe was created through sound—specifically, the sacred syllable Om (Aum). At the heart of Hindu beliefs is Brahman, the infinite, uncreated, formless Source of all that exists. Brahman is not a person, but pure consciousness, the underlying reality of everything.

"OM! This Imperishable Word is the whole of this visible Universe. Its explanation is as follows: What has become, what is becoming, what will become—verily, all of this is OM. And what is beyond these three states of the world of time—that too, verily, is OM.
—Mandukya Upanishad.

Even though religious ideas may differ on the surface, deeper reflection reveals that many revelations have been shared across times, some even long before others, often influencing one another. The idea of a hidden, all-encompassing, unknowable Divine is not new. It is part of our deepest collective memory. Across ages and cultures, the same truth continues to whisper: the Divine is beyond names, beyond doctrines, and beyond form.

"Form is emptiness; emptiness is form."
—Buddhism – Heart Sūtra

Therefore, even in their deep differences, we can recognize a universal description of the Divine. From the earliest religious writings to modern spiritual movements, through rituals and traditions—and even within systems that have been manipulated over time to serve power structures or reinforce a patriarchal image of the Divine—it is often defined and described as a mysterious, all-encompassing force: one that breathes life into existence, holds creation in order, and speaks to the heart of human consciousness. Whether we are connected to it by creation, by thought, or by inner awareness, the Divine is experienced as a source of wholeness, unconditional presence, inner wisdom, mystery, and sacred unity.

Across time and culture, this same unseen presence is often not limited by gender or form, but rather given to us, coming for us, or becoming us. And though the pathways may vary, the qualities of the Divine remain strikingly universal.

> *"All this, verily is Brahman. The Self is Brahman [...] This is the Lord of All; the Omniscient; the Indwelling Controller; the Source of All. This is the beginning and the end of all beings."*
> —Mandukya Upanishad

Across different religions and traditions, the Divine is often described as transcending logic, escaping definition, and moving beyond what the human mind can fully grasp. As human beings, our understanding is limited—shaped by language, time, and perception—while the Divine is not. It surpasses all understanding.

Therefore, we may feel its presence. We may sense its guidance. But we cannot fully comprehend its totality, for it is the mystery from which all other mysteries arise.

> *"The Tao that can be told is not the eternal Tao. The name that can be named is not the eternal name."*
> —Tao Te Ching, Chapter 1

The Source of Many Voices, but One Origin

Whether through prayer, trance, meditation, devotion, rhythm, silence, or communion with nature, the Divine is often not encountered through external rituals alone, but through an inner shift. It can be a quieting of the mind, an opening of the heart, or a surrender of control. What matters most is not the form, but the *presence*: a sense of being held, guided, or known by something greater.

Despite cultural and theological differences, one truth consistently emerges: the Divine is not distant. It is near, within, and always seeking relationship with the part of us that dares to listen.

The journey of truly knowing ourselves is just as intricate as understanding the Divine. It is not something that can be fully measured—only experienced.

Just as light passes through stained glass and takes on many colors, the Divine—though One—reveals itself in many forms. Some find comfort in structured doctrine, while others feel the Divine in nature, in music, in silence, or in moments of deep intuition. Our beliefs are often born from where we have been, what we have needed, and what we have experienced.

A person born into a desert tribe might envision the Divine as fire and wind; someone raised by the sea may speak of it as water and depth. One tradition may describe the Divine as a father, another as a mother, a force, a presence, or even a silence. That is why I believe that no single path can fully capture the whole. We all carry fragments of understanding, and together, these diverse views create a larger mosaic.

I believe the Divine is not a force that requires any external intervention to be reached. It dwells within us—guiding, sustaining, and awakening us to our true and highest Self.

It is Genesis.

It is Mirror.

It is the end of all things.

Some of us were taught that revelation ended with a book. But what if the book was never the final word? What if the Divine still speaks—through art, through silence, science, through a stranger's kindness or a dream that lingers? The Source did not stop speaking. We only stopped listening.

Science as Modern scripture

The ancient texts spoke in symbols and stars, in fire and whispers. Today, science writes in numbers and Lightwave. But the message—if one listens beyond the jargon—is also familiar.

The cosmic microwave background (CMB) is faint leftover light from the Big Bang. Think of it as a quiet song that has been playing across the universe for 13.8 billion years. Scientists call it the CMB, while mystics might say it is the first sound of creation—the sacred OM or the *"Let there be light"* hidden in static. But not all lights are visible. So, when telescopes like James Webb observe the universe, it looks beyond our human senses. It captures infrared light waves—a type of light we cannot see. This is why James Webb sees galaxies, through dust and darkness, as they existed less than 400 million years after the Big Bang.

We have then learned that the universe is filled with waves of energy—some visible, some not. Just like love. Just like thought. Just like the Divine.

We now know that as the James Webb Telescope peers back across 13 billion years of

The Source of Many Voices, but One Origin

light-travel time, it is not merely witnessing the past; it is witnessing *memory*—the universe remembering how to paint in the dark. It sees order already at play: galaxies taking shape in the cosmic dawn, assembling with astonishing grace yet always within the boundaries set by the fundamental constants. The universe behaves like a perfectly tuned instrument; if you alter one string, the entire symphony will collapse into noise. It is as if a Divine Artist were stirring first colors onto an invisible canvas—swirls of matter, bursts of radiance—where the laws of physics meet *intention*.

And what are we, if not made of that same *intention*?

Everything around and within us follows an order. The sun, the moon, the seasons, the trees, the oceans, our organs, our cells—even the tiniest molecules within us—are all at work, moving to a sacred rhythm. An order that existed long before we were born and will continue long after we leave this lifetime. It is an order greater than ourselves.

Quantum physicists speak of fields unseen, where every particle is not a thing, but a vibration. One names it quantum entanglement; the other, spiritual unity.

So then, what is science—but another spiritual tongue? A modern scripture—decoded not in temples or rituals, but in telescopes.

When we look through the Webb telescope, we are not just looking *"out"*—we are looking *within* the memory of the Source. And this becomes our invitation to stop asking whether science or spirituality is right—and start listening to the *One Voice* speaking through *All*.

Whether we call it fine-tuning, providence, or cosmic law, science itself shows that existence rests on razor-thin margins of order—margins that allow us to breathe, think, and wonder why...

The Parable of the Craft's Market

As summer drew near, a village opened its yearly festival honoring local artisans. Hundreds of visitors arrived, eager to see and buy the finest work they had ever laid their eyes on.

In the rugs' section, long rows of weavers sat shoulder-to-shoulder, each working with just one color. One wove only blue, another red, another green, yellow, pink, and so on. No hue looked the same.

A traveler approached, entranced by the beauty yet puzzled by its incompleteness.

"Goodness," she said. "Such beautiful threads! But ... why does each of you weave only one color?"

An elderly weaver, fingers-stained deep indigo, looked up and said: "Child, would you ask a rose to bloom in every shade? Each of us tends the color we know best."

A young man in a straw hat—working an eager yellow thread—leaned over and responded: "But together we are making something none of us could finish alone."

The traveler looked around. The red weaver hummed a soft tune; the blue weaver nodded in time; the yellow strand crossed them both, shimmering where it touched. Soon green appeared where blue met yellow, and violet where red kissed blue.

She turned back to the elder. "Still, wouldn't it be quicker if one of you used every color?"

"Quicker, perhaps," the elder said, eyes crinkling. "But not wiser. Weaving is more than cloth. If I tried to hold every color, the pattern would fall apart. Look at my hands—dyed indigo. How could blue carry yellow and red at once? Forcing my shade onto theirs would dull the masterpiece. Each of us works with the color already on our fingers."

A breeze rustled the canopy. The traveler noticed tiny flecks of yarn drifting in the sunlight, mingling before settling on the looms. Every strand—no matter how small—found its place.

She exhaled. "I see. The beauty is not in a single color; it is in the way they meet."

"Exactly," the yellow weaver said, tying off his row. "Here, no color is missing—because every heart that arrives brings its own hue."

The elder nodded. "No single hand can hold every thread. The masterpiece is born only when we lay our colors together."

✦ ✦ ✦

No religion or tradition contains the whole tapestry, yet each strand is indispensable. People cling to the colors that life has placed in their hands. But if the One Source belonged to just one group, why would we all breathe the same air, though from different places? Rejecting an unfamiliar color dims the brilliance of the design taking shape. True devotion does not force every thread to match; it is trusting the Weaver whose loom is far larger than our view.

When we welcome every sincere strand—scripture, song, silence, science—we discover an embroidery of meaning that no single doctrine could hold. Be the traveler who gathers colors, not the gatekeeper who hoards one hue.

Many times, we impose our beliefs on others in the name of being *"good."* Yet each of us carries colors on our hands. Some hues are gifts of tradition, culture, or family; others were pressed upon us through domination, slavery, or conquest.

Look closely at your fingertips: perhaps your colors have taught you to give thanks to nature with rhythm and dance, expressing gratitude, love, and harmony. Is that so different from the colors of someone who kneels in a temple, give thanks, and preach love? Or from the one who uses science and knowledge to reveal that—*there is indeed something*—to be grateful for? Our shades may vary, but the light they reflect is the same.

When we dismiss parts of understanding and knowledge because we are convinced that our own is the "*good*," and the only "*one*," we may also silence the very voice that could teach us more about ourselves.

CHAPTER 4

THE LIE OF HOLY PERFECTION

For a long time, I held a different understanding of the Divine. I used to believe it was only what was considered *"good"* and *"holy."* For quite a time, I rejected any thoughts or actions I had labeled as bad—without truly understanding why I was having them in the first place. I rejected them simply because I had been told they were wrong.

There was no space for self-inquiry or reflection—only rules about what was pure and impure, what to keep and what to cast away. I was not taught how to make choices that naturally aligned with who I am and the respect I hold for others. It was more about obedience than understanding, and I began to judge others through the same lens—based on my learned perception of what was *right* and *wrong*. But along my spiritual path, I have come to a deeper realization: the Divine is not limited to goodness—because the Divine is *everything*.

"We often ask, why did you do that? Or why did I act like that? We do act, and yet, everything we do is God's creative action."
—Rumi (The Essential Rumi)

We are often taught to divide life into two categories: the good and the bad. The blessing and the burden. The joy and the suffering. But what if this division is not truth—but perception?

I believe that the Divine does not obey our narrow categories of good and bad—because without what we consider bad, the concept of good would hold no meaning.

> *"I form the light and create darkness, I bring prosperity and create disaster; I, the Lord, do all these things."*
> — Isaiah 45:7 (NIV)

This is also explained in The Kybalion, a modern summary of ancient Hermetic principles— wisdom said come from Kemet (early Egypt). Principles inscribed in the Emerald Tablet of Tehuti (also known as Thoth, in later Greek and Egyptian texts, and later as Hermes Trismegistus, who was a symbol of divine intelligence and sacred language.) The Principle of Polarity explores how opposites reveal deeper unity. It explains that opposites are not enemies, but extremes of the same energy.

> *"Everything is dual; everything has poles; everything has its pair of opposites; like and unlike are the same; opposites are identical in nature, but different in degree; extremes meet [...]"*
> —The Kybalion (Principle of Polarity)

For much of my life, I was taught that "paradise" was a place where no *darkness* could exist. But now, I believe that paradise is not a location—it is a return to Self. Return that becomes possible after we embrace the *lessons* that reveal who we are.

The Lie of Holy Perfection

I believe that both light and shadow come from the Source. Not to harm us, but to teach us. Not to punish, but to awaken.

What we often call *"bad"* is simply the part of the story we do not yet understand. It is the chapter before clarity, the ache before the wisdom, the silence before the song.

And so, I start to see that holiness was never about rules of perfection—it was about presence. It was about consciousness. The presence we bring to our healing and to our contradictions.

Sometimes, the truths that free us do not arrive in sermons or sacred texts, they arrive in our own raw becoming. In that spirit, I want to offer you this:

You do not have to be flawless to be sacred.
Healing is not a straight line.
Spirit chooses wholeness, not perfection.

"True perfection seems imperfect, yet it is perfectly itself. True fullness seems empty, yet it is fully present."
—Tao Te Ching, Chapter 45

Our human understanding is shaped by time, by fear, by the need for comfort. So, when something breaks, we call it loss. When something ends, we call it failure. When someone leaves, we call it abandonment. But from the perspective of hidden understanding, these may be transitions into something greater, something more aligned with who we truly are becoming.

Therefore, to reject the darkness while only embracing the light is, in some ways, a form of resistance to the Source—and, by extension to ourselves.

Remember what we perceive as pain is often a doorway to discovery. What we label as hurtful is sometimes the birthplace of transformation, and what we see as a curse can become an invitation to become something more.

The idea that only the *"good"* comes from the Divine can be misleading, because the Divine is limitless in what it can create, teach and transform.

Just as *yin* and *yang* embody the balance of polarities, *Ifá* offers a parallel insight. Ifá is an African spirituality that is practiced among Yoruba communities and throughout the African diaspora in the Americas and the Caribbean. Within this tradition, Divine love is the artisan who sculpts with shadow and light at once:

"Tribulation does not come without its blessings; the good and the bad are always together."
— Holy Odu Iwori-Ósé

In Ifá spirituality every destiny carries both *ìrẹ̀* (blessing) and *ibi* (challenge), sacred gifts intended to cultivate balanced character. The verse reminds us that adversity is never punishment; it is an equal partner to sweetness. Accepting both as sacred prevents spiritual arrogance and dissolves the myth that life must be *"perfect."* Perfect in the sense that we are taught to define it.

African spirituality thus joins Taoism (*balance of the yin and yang*), Buddhism (*Heart Sūtra:* "Form is emptiness; emptiness is form*), Hinduism (*Bhagavad Gītā 7:12: "The three states of material existence— goodness (sattva), passion (rajas), and darkness (tamas)— are manifested by My energy. They are in Me, yet I am beyond them."*), and the Hermetic spirituality (*law of polarity*)—in declaring that light and shadow flow from one Source for the soul's refinement. By removing the illusion of flawless holiness, the scriptures invite seekers to welcome pain and

The Lie of Holy Perfection

pleasure alike as sacred teachers.

Even Christian teaching reflects this balance in Jesus's embrace of both joy and suffering. The teaching was never to accept the *good* while rejecting the *bad*, but to hold them together to understand sacred purpose more deeply.

When circumstances shift, we often assume that something has gone *wrong* or that *"the devil"* is causing pain; yet without such trials we cannot grow into the fullness of our becoming.

Just as we accept the balance of opposing forces on a grand scale, we must also apply that principle to our personal lives, recognizing that every choice shapes what lies ahead. Self-knowledge and connection to the Divine reveal a simple truth: *every part of us carries meaning, and true harmony rests in balancing them.* Therefore, cultivating introspection by truly examine our habits, actions, and thoughts is to accept and understand our many "*colors*," not out of self-judgment or fear of a deity who might punish, but out of a sincere desire to live in balanced wholeness.

Seeing situations through a spiritual lens also allows you to stop judging by your own understanding or logic. It invites you to forgive and let go of what is incomprehensible, knowing that everything is happening for your highest good and the highest good of all—because we are all connected.

Don't you know that some parents have watched their children die—not out of punishment, but because through that deep sorrow, they were transformed? Not necessarily into someone "better" or "worse"—but into someone different. Someone grown.

We are here to grow. We are here to learn. Have you remained in the same infant form you were born in? Did your learning stop the moment you entered this world? No—you are in constant transformation: physically, emotionally, and spiritually.

Don't you know that entire civilizations have vanished, and nations have gone to war—not without purpose, but perhaps because new souls needed to be born elsewhere, in different parts of the world... or even beyond it?

Let me share with you how pain became my teacher: I was born with sickle cell disease—a condition that brings intense physical pain and suffering. Among my four siblings—all from the same parents—I was the only one born with it. As a child, I remember understanding that it was emotionally heartbreaking for my parents to watch their child endure so much pain, knowing they were powerless to change it. There was no cure. No easy answer.

I had to learn to live with it, and, I had to learn to pray to be healed. In our Christian home, prayer was the first response to everything, especially suffering on circumstances that we do not have the power to change.

As a child, I often asked myself:
"Why am I cursed?"
"Why am I the one suffering like this?"
"What did I do to deserve such punishment?"

When the pain was in my leg, I would beg for it to be cut off, just to have it removed from my body. I cried. Sometimes, I could not even walk. I would crawl across the floor just to reach something if no one was there to help me. I was suffering.

But let me tell you my truth now: Because of this pain, I learned how to encourage others. Because of this disease, I learned how to love

The Lie of Holy Perfection

myself more and balance my life. Because of these long, painful nights, I learned how to listen and to communicate with the deepest part of myself.

For a long time, I searched for healing only by looking at what was happening on a physical level. But healing did not come that way. At least, not in the form I was expecting.

If you are asking yourself: "How can I stay positive when everything around me is chaos?" I will respond this to you: "But what if it is not chaos?"

The reason you see it that way is because you have labeled it as chaos—and attached to that label all the negative definitions you have learned. But, when you shift to a spiritual perspective, there is no chaos. No tragedy. No senseless suffering. There are only lessons—opportunities to reconnect with the inner self and, therefore, your truest self.

The question to ask is not: "Why is this happening to me?"; but rather: "What is this here to teach me, knowing that everything is interconnected?"

Yes—everything is interconnected.

On a micro level, think about your own life. How every experience—*good* or *bad*—has shaped who you are today.

Now, expand that to a macro level. The same is true for the world we live in.

Nations have fallen; others have risen. Populations have shifted. Empires have vanished; new ones have emerged. It is all part of an eternal transformation—a sacred dance of destruction and rebirth.

A motivational teacher would tell you that success is shaped by the consistent actions that you take every day. In other words, what you see in the macro exists first in the micro. Therefore, all planes of existence are reflections of each other—the micro reflects the macro.

> *"As above, so below; as within, so without."*
> —The Kybalion (Principle of Correspondence)

This ancient Kemetic principle reminds us that the micro and the macro, the inner and outer, are always mirroring each other.

> *"Everything is enfolded into everything."*
> —David Bohm, quantum physicist

Within each of us, we carry both what we consider as light and shadow. I came to understand that those concepts are shaped by where we were born, the century, the culture, the belief system we inherited. What is considered "good" or "bad" is not universal truth. That's why laws change. Doctrines evolve. People grow.

The less we come to know ourselves, the more we establish external rules to govern our thoughts and behavior. The less we know ourselves, the more disconnected we become from the unseen forces, and connected to the rules we create—rules that often lead to division, judgment, and oppression.

Someone may oppose me and argue that "what's bad is bad, and what's good is good." But I have come to understand that this perspective exists only on the physical plane. Now, I see that—*everything belongs to the unfolding*.

All the unseen forces around us do not wait a single moment. Every experience—joyful or painful—is a thread in the tapestry of your becoming. And even when you cannot see the pattern, know this: *Everything is unfolding; and*

The Lie of Holy Perfection

everything belongs.

The purpose of our learning here goes beyond the physical world. Let's learn to recognize when we are in the middle of a *personal* or *global* transformation.

When empires carried a foreign god to new lands to serve power, that god often arrived with *legal codes, contracts, rules, and weapons.* The promise of salvation masked an exchange: spiritual obedience in return for political submission. Inner knowledge and symbols were often demonized so that the imposed faith, rules and laws could appear to be the lone cure for a sickness that outsiders themselves had defined. A way of saying: *"You lack the true path; we will fix you."*

Thus, the inhabitants of these lands often learn to measure their worth against an imported ideal that ignores their history, skin, language, or gender roles. A covert message lingers: *"If you wish to be holy and good—be like us."*

With these shifts in connection to the Divine—and the rise of new belief systems and adaptations—people have grown hesitant to trust their dreams, inner guidance, ancestral wisdom, or direct mystical insight. For a very long time, any personal or natural inquiry into the unseen was punished, as the Divine was confined to a single path and positioned on a distant throne, accessed only through appointed intermediaries.

✦ ✦ ✦

Story of the Bitter Cure
"Swallow this medicine—it is good for you."

There was once a valley where every child was born holding a small, clear vial. Inside each vial shimmered a living spark that the elders called *the*

Inner Light. When villagers faced doubt, they warmed the vial in their palms, closed their eyes, and listened. In dreams, in quiet intuitions, in sudden bursts of color behind the eyelids, the Light offered counsel. Thus, the valley thrived—no palace, no prison—just footpaths bordered by clay shrines and painted walls where people honored the Source they felt within.

One season a great Empire arrived. Its banners were bright, its drums unceasing, and its priests carried heavy chests filled with scrolls, contracts, and iron tablets etched with foreign laws. At the center of their procession rode an enormous apothecary cart. Inside the cart sat a single obsidian urn sealed with wax.

The chief priest dismounted and spoke: "People of this valley, you suffer a sickness you cannot see. Your dreams deceive you, your tiny vials are weak. There is only one connection to God, and he has sent a medicine to save you. Drink it and you shall be safe forever, as you have been practicing what is evil and bad. If you don't obey, you shall be punished."

The villagers hesitated. The priest, perceiving their doubt, produced lists of forbidden behaviors, fines for disobedience, and shiny coins as rewards for compliance. Soldiers demonstrated the sharpness of their spears. Merchants displayed textiles stamped with imperial symbols. Seeing the valley was unarmed, the villagers surrendered their vials and lined up to drink the medicine.

The liquid was acrid—throats burned, eyes watered, bellies twisted. Yet the priests insisted, "Endure the bitterness—it proves the cure is working."

Shortly after, a big temple was built with precious stones that the villagers were forced to

The Lie of Holy Perfection

give, and a golden throne was placed behind its gates. Only certified intermediaries might approach the throne; everyone else could plead for forgiveness from a distance.

The villagers were required to ask forgiveness for every action or any thought. They had to live in constant penitence, convinced they were only sinners. They were instructed to abandon any search for other truth or connection with the Divine—and even with themselves. A single lesson was pressed upon them: *instead of knowing they were light, they must now accept that they were nothing but "dust."*

Years passed. Children were now born without vials, for the practice had been forgotten. Dreams were dismissed as idle nonsense, intuition as unreliable emotion. Each day, villagers inspected one another for impurities of dress, diet, thoughts and speech. Any shadow of grief or anger was labeled evil and punished with public penance. In their quest for outward perfection, they began to fear one another's *imperfections*.

A quiet midwife named Kaona broke one such rule. She awoke from a vivid dream in which a river of light poured from her own chest, restoring a dying tree to bloom. Overwhelmed, she told her neighbor, and word reached the clergy. For claiming direct contact with the Divine, she was condemned to silence. Alone in a stone cell, she recalled forgotten stories of the vials and the *Inner Light*. With nothing to lose, she placed a hand over her heart and listened. The same warm current rose, gentle and unmistakable.

When her sentence ended, Kaona walked to the village market at midday and spoke loudly: "The cure we continue to swallow numbed the illness that never existed, and in numbing us it stole half our senses. The Light has never left the heart. It is still within us."

At first the crowd mocked her, for fear breeds quick ridicule. But an old potter stepped forward. He remembered that his grandmother once hummed lullabies about sparks in glass. A child admitted she heard colors talking in dreams. Small confessions rippled through the market. That evening, villagers gathered without priests and shared forgotten dreams. Some wept, tasting sweetness behind long-suppressed grief. Others felt anger, but it rang like a drum, driving them to honest action rather than shame.

Word spread. People began leaving the temple gates unlocked, approaching the golden throne without intermediaries, discovering it merely gilded wood. They retrieved their vials—many cracked, some empty—and found the Light rekindled the moment they believed it could. The empire's officials, seeing their grip loosen, declared the valley rebellious and withdrew their garrisons in search of softer lands.

The villagers kept the obsidian urn at the edge of the square as a reminder. Below it, they carved an inscription:

"Bitter medicine may quiet the body, but it cannot heal the soul. All natural insight, consciousness, and spiritual awareness are given as gifts—not to punish, but to help us live in harmony with our true self. Shadow and light are both daughters of one Source, reminding us that life itself operates through balance, rebirth and transformation; to reject either is to reject the whole."

Once you embrace this awareness, you will be ready to reclaim what you once disowned. As you reclaim it, you begin to see every version and aspect of who you truly are.

CHAPTER 5

THE THREE REALMS OF BEING

When I was a teenager, I became fascinated by psychology and started reading everything I could about the soul and the mind. I wanted to understand, in some ways, the deeper layers of being: the body, the soul, and the spirit. I was trying to make sense of things I was experiencing, hoping to find logic in the unseen.

In high school, we had a basic psychology class that introduced me to some ideas of the three layers of Self, such as the conscious, subconscious and unconscious mind.

That class sparked something in me, but what truly expanded my understanding were my unexpected out-of- body experiences.

An out-of-body experience—often abbreviated as OBE—is a phenomenon where a person perceives themselves as existing outside of their physical body. During such episodes, individuals often report seeing their own body from an external vantage point, or traveling to distant places, realms, or dimensions. While science often classifies OBEs under altered states of consciousness, various spiritual traditions consider them natural occurrences that can arise spontaneously or be cultivated through practices like deep meditation, breathwork, or astral projection.

It was not the books or the lectures that brought me clarity, but what I lived.

✦ ✦ ✦

My first out-of-body experience:

At the time, I did not even know what it was—or how to name it. I was in my early teens, probably around 12 or 13 years old. I was sick and was resting in my parents' bed. For some reason, when I was unwell, I often liked to sleep in a bed that was not my own to feel better—usually in my parents' or even my brothers' room—especially during the day or the afternoon.

It was around 7 p.m. I remember it clearly.

Suddenly, I found myself standing next to the bed, looking at my own body sleeping. I could hear my father in the living room speaking to a neighbor who had come to visit. The master bedroom was next to the living room, so I walked over. I saw my father sitting on the accent chair by the TV, and the neighbor was seated on the chair that faced the lobby room.

I remember the neighbor wearing a pale blue t-shirt with two navy blue stripes across the front. They were talking about a soccer game. My father asked him if he wanted something to drink; he declined, saying he'd be heading home soon.

Then, just as suddenly, I returned to the bedroom. A short time later, I woke up.

I stayed in bed, reflecting on what I had seen. I felt better, so I got up and went to the living room. My father was still there. I told him what had happened.

The Three Realms of Being

He tried to offer a logical explanation. Since the bedroom was close to the living room, and I was likely in a light sleep, maybe I had overheard the conversation and dreamt about it.

That made sense—until I described the scene. I told him exactly where he and the neighbor had been sitting and pointed out the navy stripes on the neighbor's t-shirt. The door to the bedroom had been closed, and by the time I woke up, the neighbor was already gone. There was no way I could have seen those details from where I had been lying.

My father looked at me with a familiar expression—a slow nod, raised eyebrows, deep in thought. "Well," he said, "I think it's because you are tired and sick. Sometimes, when you are unwell, your dreams can feel very different."

And that was it. We never spoke about it again—not with my father, not with anyone.

As my father explained, I learned later that from a scientific and psychological perspective, OBEs are often seen as the brain entering a unique neurological or cognitive state—usually triggered by extreme stress, fatigue, trauma, or intense focus. But my second experience reveals something deeper...

The second experience is the one that truly made me understand the three realms of being or *triple architecture of the self.* It happened with my little sister Synthia, and I believe it's an experience neither of us will ever forget.

To better explain this experience, I will use the terms body, soul, and spirit. The body represents my physical, sleeping self; the soul represents the invisible part of me that resides within the body; and the spirit is the conscious, unseen aspect of myself that was outside—seeing, understanding, and guiding through this OBE.

At the time, my sister and I shared a bedroom at our parents' home. One night, my spirit suddenly found itself outside of the body, looking down at my sleeping self. I saw my sister getting out of her bed and walking to the outlet near the door to plug in her phone. She sat on the floor and began checking her messages. My spirit moved next to her and could clearly see what she was doing.

Shortly after, my spirit turned and looked at my body lying on the bed and decided to communicate with it.

In that moment, it felt as though my spirit was communicating with an invisible part of me. Even though I was looking at my physical body, I was, in fact, communicating with my soul—within the body.

The conversation between my spirit and my soul was purely telepathic. Like we could understand each other mentally. But also, it feels like my spirit could not directly communicate with my body without the intervention of my soul.

"Ask your sister to wake you up," my spirit said to my soul within the sleeping body.

My soul did not respond in words I could hear, but I understood that it gave a command to my body—to try to speak while asleep, to call out to my sister and let her know to wake me up.

"Synthia, wake me up." I said.

From my out-of-body perspective, my spirit saw my sister pause and glance toward my bed, still seated on the floor. She looked confused, as if unsure whether she had really heard me.

"Ask her again." My spirit said.

The Three Realms of Being

Through the same inner process—my soul gives order to my sleeping body to repeat the message.

My sister finally got up and shook me until I woke up. At this moment I came back to myself.

"What is wrong with you?" My sister said.

She was visibly upset. She explained how it had scared her. My eyes and mouth had remained closed, yet she heard me calling her. The voice was muffled and eerie—not because it wasn't real, but because I was trying to push through clenched teeth, as if I was intentionally speaking, without being awake.

"How could you even see I was there? You were sleeping with your eyes closed!" She said.

I tried to explain. I told her I had left my body and saw that she was awake, sitting on the floor with her phone. I needed her to wake me up.

"I needed you to wake me up. For some reason, I could not get back to myself..."

"You could not get back to yourself?" she replied, frustrated. "What if I hadn't been there? I don't know what kind of experiences you are trying to have but leave me out of it. I don't like it!"

Understandably, she asked me not to do that to her again. Of course, it hadn't been intentional. But this experience changed my understanding of reality forever.

Firstly, the telepathic conversation between my spirit and soul was nothing that I experienced before, yet profoundly real. I could see everything—even with my eyes closed—sensing the surroundings and had a clear understanding of the situation. For the first time I experienced the connection between a part of myself that could see beyond the physical, and that was also able to communicate with another invisible part of me that resides within my body. This experience confirmed for me that I was more than flesh.

Secondly, trying to speak from within the body while "sleeping" felt incredibly difficult. The best way I can describe it, is that it felt like speaking underwater. Strangely, I could feel a kind of "energy" moving through me as I tried to form words—as if some sort of force was leaving me, and every word required intense effort.

It felt like the effort came directly from my lungs and breath.

Also, I understood something profound: the body is only the visible, physical vessel—the shell through which we move and feel. It reacts to the soul, while the spirit is the higher awareness.

This spirit—what I now recognize as my inner voice—has never been outside of me. It lives within me. And in moments of deep stillness or rest, it can temporarily leave the body and remain in communication with the soul.

The soul acts like a witness, closely connected to the body and the spirit. It is like a bridge connecting them together. It carries short-term memories, beliefs, and emotional imprints. The soul is what I call the breathing mind—the soft, witnessing awareness that lives between thought and feeling, always connected to the body, always listening. That is why you can feel something *deeply in your soul.*

But what I often call "intuition"—I now believe is the spirit guiding me. It holds deep awareness beyond our immediate perception. It is free. It is learning. It is us.

My third out-of-body experience happened recently, at home, at the beginning of 2025, and it was one of the reasons I thought of my previous experiences again.

I suddenly found myself lying next to my own body on my bed. I could see myself sleeping, and I remember thinking, "It's been a long time since this has happened. What should I do with it?"

As I looked at my body, I began telepathically communicating with my soul once again. We both had the thought: What if I tried to visit my family in another country? It felt possible. But as I began to move through the living room, I suddenly felt like I could not leave my sleeping-self.

It was not fear in the usual sense; it was more like a wave of compassion. A pull. I still can't fully explain it, but I went back to bed and re-entered my body. I woke up immediately afterward.

Lying there, I took a moment to speak to myself in silence. I thanked all parts of my being:

I thanked my body for being a home to rest in. My soul for witnessing the moments and showing compassion. And my spirit, for reconnecting me to my true Self.

Then I gently drifted back to sleep.

These experiences did not just show me something out of the ordinary, they taught me that we are designed to operate on multiple levels at once. Our reality is not only physical. It is layered—and when we understand those layers, we return to the truth of who we are.

Have you noticed how I used "I" to describe the part that left the body? It comes very naturally to me—I do not know what else to call it, because it feels like the *real* me. Strangely, the body feels like something *outside* of me. If anyone has ever experienced an out-of-body experience, they have likely felt the same. But in truth, if in every OBE, I know that I am not the body I see sleeping, but the invisible part that is living the experience—then who am I, truly?

I grew up in Christian traditions, so I knew that out-of-body experiences are often viewed with caution or skepticism. While the Bible includes mystical visions and spiritual encounters—such as Paul's account knowing someone that being "caught up to the third heaven" (2 Corinthians 12:2-5)—many contemporary interpretations have distanced themselves from such experiences, especially when they fall outside the boundaries of accepted doctrine. For some, OBEs may be associated with the occult, New Age practices, or even deception, leading believers to fear or reject them altogether.

> *I know a man in Christ who fourteen years ago was caught up to the third heaven. Whether it was in the body or out of the body I do not know—God knows. ³ And I know that this man—whether in the body or apart from the body I do not know, but God knows— ⁴ was caught up to paradise and heard inexpressible things, things that no one is permitted to tell. ⁵ I will boast about a man like that, but I will not boast about myself, except about my weaknesses.*
> —2 Corinthians 12:2-5 (NIV)

For a long time, I feared these experiences because they did not fit into the framework I was taught to trust. I could not really talk to someone that could give me a clear explanation about the spiritual changes that I was experiencing. As a teenager, if I talked about it, I was quickly told it was a dark and harmful practice, even though I was not practicing anything, but simply experiencing what was happening to me. Therefore, I had learned to associate spiritual safety with obedience to external rules and, not with inner exploration. So when the second experience happened, it brought me both wonder and discomfort. I knew that I was encountering something unknown, but at the same time, I was also confronting a part of myself that perhaps I needed to bury.

I later understood that sometimes, experience speaks louder than doctrine. My experiences would not leave me. They were part of my past and part of what I knew about myself. Burying them would not change the fact that they had taught me I was more than flesh—they taught me that an unseen part of me had the ability to exist beyond the physical realm, to communicate telepathically, and to make me see even with my eyes closed. Therefore, for me, it was no longer something I should be afraid of, but something that revealed knowledge about my own existence, identity, and connection to something greater.

When we open ourselves to the vastness of who we are—without fear—we give permission to the unseen to reveal itself. It is the hidden part of us that already knows the truth. This is why, when you want to give up on a project, that insistent inner compass keeps urging you to keep going.

Even if you abandon a dream for years, the moment you allow yourself to rest, to reflect, to reconnect through introspection, silence or meditation—those forgotten dreams resurface, like an old version of you gently returning, asking to be seen and *be born* again.

A true calling does not let you rest. You can try to walk away, but your inner voice will speak until it is fulfilled—because it truly knows you. And when that calling is honored, something profound in you will begin to show you visions... dreams... projects to birth... And each one brings you a deep sense of peace.

That is how you know you are no longer being driven by what the world demands of you—but by a higher purpose. A purpose you can *feel*, even when it cannot yet be seen.

> *"There is nothing in the world but what is seen of the mind itself [...]."*
> —The Lankavatara Sutra.

> *"He has also set eternity in the human heart."*
> —Ecclesiastes 3:11

> *"[...] The Kingdom of God is within you and outside you of you. Whoever knows himself will discover this. [...]*
> —Gospel of Thomas, verse 3.

This is a reminder that you are more than what you can see. Some teachers have explained that we are mental beings—which, to me, hold the same meaning as being spiritual. It suggests that our experiences and realizations in this physical world operate first on a mental or spiritual level.

As explained in metaphysical teachings, like the Kybalion and the Silva Method (a meditation system combining mind training and intuition), the mind is seen as the origin of all creation—not merely as thought, but as spiritual essence. In these teachings, being "mental" is synonymous with being aligned to the spiritual blueprint of life.

The Three Realms of Being

"You are not a human being with a mind. You are a mind using a human body."
—José Silva, The Sila Mind Control Method

This mirrors ancient Kemetic wisdom. Kemet, the ancient spiritual heart of Egypt, believed creation began with consciousness itself. It was taught and referred in the Kybalion that the Divine is mental.

"The All is mental."
—The Kybalion

But also the Lankavatara Sutra teachings about the mind:

"The beginning lies in the recognition that the external world is only a manifestation of the activities of the mind. [...] They do not recognize that the objective world rises from the mind itself; they do not understand that the whole mind-system also arises from the mind itself."

Teaching may evolve across time and cultures, but the truth behind them is never lost—only remembered.
Spirit remembers.
Soul witnesses.
Body expresses.
You are the bridge between worlds—the one who remembers, the one who witnesses, the one who becomes.
I am aware that not all spiritual paths use the terms "spirit" and "soul" in the way I have. Some traditions may speak only of *consciousness*, describing it as the totality of who we are—without separation or inner distinctions. In certain

teachings, the soul and the spirit are not seen as different aspects, but as illusions created by the mind. Instead, the focus is on pure awareness, the unchanging presence that observes all experiences without identifying with them.

I honor those perspectives deeply. My use of the terms "spirit" and "soul" comes from the language I grew up with and the way I first learned to understand myself. These words helped me give form to what I was feeling and experiencing, especially during moments that could not be explained logically. For me, they remain meaningful. They allow me to name the parts of myself that witness, that remember, that guide, and that evolve.

At the same time, I remain open. I do not believe there is only one way to speak about the unseen. What one tradition calls the "soul," another may call the "psyche," "higher self," "light body," or simply "awareness." These are not contradictions, but reflections of a shared truth viewed through different lenses. The divine, after all, can wear many names and reveal itself through many paths.

So, while I may use familiar words rooted in my upbringing, I carry no attachment to be "right." I write with the hope that others, too, may find their own language to describe the mystery within. Because what truly matters is not what we call it—but that we seek to know it. To know ourselves. To open the door to the invisible and walk with wonder toward the truth of our being by removing all illusion of separation.

CHAPTER 6

THE ILLUSION OF SEPARATION

When I was a teenager, I won the crown in my high school pageant. I remember stepping on stage to introduce myself: my name, my grade, and why I deserved to win.

My class had selected me to represent them, and in the two weeks leading up to the championship day, all the candidates had to undergo walking training. We practiced our posture, our communication, our smiles. We reviewed our dresses, our heels, our makeup. We even studied for possible questions—ranging from general knowledge to science and history.

At first, it was something I did for fun. But that changed quickly. For the first time, I witnessed people I did not even know cheering for me, proud of me, believing in me—not only because of what I had done, but also because they saw something in me. *It felt good.* What had begun as a lighthearted experience turned into something deeply personal. I wanted to win—not so much for myself, but for them. For my classmates, my friends, my family, my teachers, and even for strangers who had chosen to believe in me. I wanted to prove that they were *right*.

From an early age, I learned to be competitive

and to define myself through labels—the same ones that had followed me all my life.

From the outside, people often assumed I was that kind of girl—the one who loved fashion and dreamed of crowns and runways. And maybe I could have been. After high school, I received offers to model and to represent Haiti in international pageants. But I said no—not out of ingratitude, but because something inside me always whispered that I belonged to a different path. A path I could not yet name, but one that slowly began to reveal itself to me, little by little.

From the moment we are born, labels are placed on us: "Smart" or "slow." "Good" or "bad." "Nice" or "naughty." "Ugly" or "beautiful." These early words become the first mirrors in which we see ourselves—not as who we are, but as others project us to be. They somehow seek to influence the voice within us and often create inner conflict between what we think, what we hear, what we see, and what we expect ourselves to be.

These projections are not always malicious, but they are limiting. They anchor us into a version of ourselves we feel obligated to perform; and unless we awaken, we risk spending a lifetime playing roles that were never truly ours.

Now, walking a spiritual path, I have come to understand that these labels are more than descriptors—they are *"distractions."*

Distractions not in the usual sense of noise or chaos but in the deeper sense of pulling our awareness away from who we truly are.

These distractions are anything that pulls our attention away from our eternal self and toward an illusion—especially the illusion of separation.

These distractions shape how we see ourselves and others—not as whole beings, but as categories:

The Illusion of Separation

race, gender, nationality, complexion, social status, etc. As we stop seeing the person behind the label.

When we forget who we are, we begin to focus on everything else we are not.

It is like driving a car: if you become too focused on your phone, the radio, or what someone else is doing on the road, you increase your risk of crashing. The same thing is happening in the world—just on a soul level.

The distractions of the world are so loud, and they have been echoing for so long, that we have become strangers to our own essence.

A label is not our truth—it is an interpretation. It is how the world tries to define the unseen by what it sees, not what it senses.

The more we use those labels—even unconsciously—the more we amplify our perception of separation. We are conditioned to gravitate toward those who look like us, speak like us, worship like us, or think like us—because similarity makes us feel safe. But that safety is often an illusion.

Many of us inherited stories of distant, watching deities—beings who reward obedience and punish defiance, who promise to enslave other nations and claim their lands as inheritance. But, as we awaken, some of us begin to feel a different presence. One that whispers instead of commands. One that invites instead of demands. Not above us—but within us.

Imagine, just for a moment, what the world might look like if we were raised to see others not by their labels, but as fellow beings of light on their own sacred mission. If instead of noticing race, status, or belief first, we noticed their presence. Their essence. Wouldn't it be easier to accept... to understand... and maybe even to love?

Unfortunately, whether consciously or unconsciously, we place people into boxes built from our experiences, education, fears, culture and ego. The ego thrives in the illusion of separation. It wants to protect itself, define itself, and often assert superiority over others. But when the ego leads, it narrows our view. It turns life into a competition and relationship into transaction.

In contrast, the inner self seeks connection, resonance, and remembrance. The more we feed the ego with separation, the further we drift from our soul's truth; from the knowing that we are already whole, and that wholeness is not exclusive, but shared.

The distraction is so loud that we begin to hate an entire group of people simply because of the country they were born in. It's so loud that we find ourselves beating, torturing, and even killing others—simply because they do not look like us; they do not think like us. It happened 500 years ago, and even earlier in history; and it is still happening again and again. These actions and mentalities reveal a troubling pattern in humanity's understanding of itself, and, by extension, its connection to the unseen.

Let's pause for a moment. *Who are we?*

Think about that deeply and ask yourself today: *Who am I?*

If I have the right to be on this planet today, why would I not recognize that same right for someone else?

If I truly believe that I am here—whether or not my purpose is fully understood—should I not also honor and respect every other creation, even when

The Illusion of Separation

I do not fully understand it?

Because *my* truth is: To reject another soul is to reject a reflection of ourselves. And to love another soul, even silently, is to remember who we truly are. Because when we remove all the labels and take off all the armor, what's left is the same: We all experience love, pain, kindness, fear, and compassion. We all need the same organs to survive. We all need oxygen. We are all warmed by the same sun and guided by the same moon. We all benefit from what nature gives freely—without judgment, without preference. Even without going into a deep spiritual analysis, purely from a physiological perspective, we are the same. We are human. We are one.

Today, I feel called to remind you that many of the divisions in our world come from the labels we carry and from our refusal to see others as reflections of ourselves. These distractions often pull us away from our inner connection. The more we sharpen our judgmental eye, the more the true compass within us begins to quiet, as the voice of the ego takes up space in the mind.

The inner compass is light. It flows gently with no hate, no fear, and no need to prove anything. So when your thoughts begin to shift toward preferences, categories, separation, or hate that is the moment to pause and ask whether there is an external voice shaping your mentality and thoughts.

My personal analysis has concluded that humanity's greatest tragedies and most violent conflicts often stemmed from one concept: *difference*.

Difference in religion. Difference in race.

Difference in belief, origin, identity, or opinion, etc.

This is not just a personal or spiritual insight—it is a pattern repeated in history. Humanity's most painful chapters often begin with one idea: *They are not like us.* Here are just a few moments where difference became division...

Conflict	Period	Rooted in Difference
The Crusades	1095–1291	Christian vs Muslim religious conflict
European Wars of Religion	1522–1648	Protestant vs Catholic divisions
The Atlantic Slave Trade	16th–19th centuries	Dehumanization based on race
American Civil War	1861–1865	Ideological split over race and slavery
World War II (Holocaust)	1939–1945	Nazi belief in Aryan supremacy
Apartheid (South Africa)	1948–1994	Racial segregation and domination

These are just a few examples—and history holds countless more. So many lives lost, so much pain and destruction... all in the name of "difference."

The more we label people, the more we amplify our perception of separation, and the more we cling to separation, the easier it becomes to fear, reject, or even hate what we don't understand.

The Illusion of Separation

But here is a spiritual truth I have come to embrace: To truly know ourselves, we must begin to see ourselves in others. By recognizing the same essence in others, we come closer to knowing who we truly are.

When we do, the lines begin to blur. Race becomes human expression. Religion becomes spiritual path. Nationality becomes circumstance, not character. And love—real love—can finally begin to flow.

Separation causes suffering, and suffering creates defense mechanisms. What looks like arrogance may be fear. What sounds like hate may be grief. If we could see the wound beneath the armor, we might respond differently. Not with agreement—but with understanding. Not with approval—but with compassion. Because behind every mask is a soul that longs to be seen.

> *" He who sees all being in the Self, and the Self in all beings, feels no revulsion [...]"*
> —Isha Upanishad verse 6.

If you truly want to be in harmony with your inner self, it is important to acknowledge the distractions that weaken your connection to your inner compass—especially the habit of labeling yourself and others. Sincerely, you cannot walk a spiritual path rooted in truth if you are still holding tightly to the illusions of separation.

What labels have you accepted that may no longer serve your truth? What assumptions have you held about others based on theirs?

The world conditions us to see others through filters. These filters are loud. They shout at us from media, tradition, and even family systems. And over time, we begin to believe that these filters are real. But they are not. Not fully.

Spirituality invites you to peel those layers away—not because identity isn't important, but because identity is not the whole story.

Labels are external. Your spirit is eternal.

If you are truly seeking alignment with your higher self, you must be willing to look beyond what divides you from others. We are all part of the same Source. Even the people you fear, ignore, or judge. To walk a spiritual path is to recognize that the same unseen energy is in everyone, even when the form it comes in, is different from your own.

Understand this today:
Distraction keeps you from seeing yourself.
Labels keep you from seeing others.
And both keep you from seeing the Divine.

This is why we must talk about it. To wake up, we must first understand what puts us to sleep. And nothing puts us to sleep faster than the illusion that being different means being divided.

In today's world, media magnifies the illusion. Algorithms feed us only what aligns with our existing beliefs. News headlines highlight division. Films portray stereotypes. Social media turns human experience into labels and hashtags. We consume these distortions until they become our truths. But spiritual awakening requires discernment. It is not about denying the world—but seeing through it. You must ask: Who benefits from this illusion? And who might I become if I stopped believing it?

CHAPTER 7

THE SACRED LAW OF DIVERSITY

What if diversity was not just natural, but spiritual; not a political stance; not a social trend—but a sacred design embedded into the very fabric of existence?

From galaxies to genes, creation never repeats itself. No leaf is copied. No snowflakes duplicated. Diversity is not disorder.

If my personal reflection has led me to believe that humanity's greatest tragedies and most violent conflicts often originated from one concept: *difference*. In this chapter, I will explain that difference was never the problem. Division was. And division is created when we are not respecting or in harmony with the sacred law of diversity.

What do you think of the universe, of nature, of everything that surrounds you? Have you ever taken a moment to notice how many breeds of dogs exist, all in different shapes, sizes, and colors? And that's just dogs.

What about ants? There are currently far more ants on this planet than humans—and they exist in approximately 13,000 known species. Now, think about the animals that fly, swim, or walk the earth. Why are there so many types—so much diversity?

The answer to me is simple: Diversity is Divine.

Take a moment and reflect on the flowers you have seen, the fruits you have tasted, the landscapes you have traveled through. None are exactly the same.

Difference is not random. Difference is sacred.

Have you ever thought of the differences that you once feared or rejected? Have you ever thought of the real wall that keeps you from accepting them?

Today, I am here to remind you that everything is created with unique intentions. Beauty itself lives in that variety. Nothing in the universe was made to be identical. From colors, shapes, languages, accents, textures, rhythms—creation celebrates contrast.

The Divine Source—or whatever name you give it—never created just one flower, one color, one season or one animal. The universe itself is a masterpiece of variety. Why then do we fear what is different from us? The truth is, we have been conditioned—generation after generation—to believe that sameness equals safety, and difference equal threat. But that belief is not spiritual. It's fearful; and fear is not the voice of the soul.

Diversity is a signature of the Divine. It is sacred. It is not a mistake—it is intentional design.

Every face you meet carries a fragment of truth. Every culture holds a piece of the divine mosaic. Every belief, even if different from yours, may still lead someone home to love, just through another door.

You do not have to agree with everyone. You do not have to become like everyone. But there is a spiritual understanding that allows you to see others with compassion. To understand that we are

The Sacred Law of Diversity

not separate beings fighting for space.

Recently, I was reading about the laws of the universe as taught by various authors.

In my spiritual journey, I have explored the Law of Karma, the Law of Vibration, the Law of Attraction, the Law of Polarity, the Law of Correspondence, the Law of Compensation, the Law of Divine Oneness, and more. But something caught my attention: None of the books I encountered listed diversity as one of these universal laws; or perhaps my research was simply limited.

Out of curiosity, I even searched online. The only reference I found to a "universal law of diversity" came from legal frameworks—through UNESCO and the Universal Declaration of Human Rights. In our current understanding, diversity is better known as a legal principle than a spiritual one. And yet, the more I reflect on the complexity and intentionality of creation, the more I believe this truth: Diversity is a spiritual law—we have just forgotten it.

However, the spirit of Hermetic philosophy, which comes from Tehuti, does imply that all things—light and shadow, masculine and feminine, above and below, visible and unseen—are different aspects of the One. In that sense, diversity is not separate from the Divine—it is an expression of it.

> *"The All is One, and the One manifests in All."*
> —Hermetic Principle

But it does not contain the phrase "diversity is divine," nor does it explicitly say anything about diversity in the way we use the term today (i.e., cultural, racial, or gender, etc.)

Perhaps one day, I will write another book

titled: "The Spiritual Law of Diversity as a Universal Law." For now, I will offer a few seeds, not from a legal lens, but from the very essence of my understanding of who we are.

Just like every other aspect of creation, we are also diverse. Understanding this principle allows us to see ourselves and others not through judgment or comparison, but through the lens of the soul. Through the eyes of divine design.

With that said, I firmly believe that nothing is meant to be exactly the same. Uniformity becomes confusing when we understand that diversity is divine. I also believe that failing to recognize this principle has cost humanity dearly.

Truly—is anything in nature ever meant to be singular?

In nature, singularity is an illusion. Even when something appears to be singular, it is known to be part of a greater pattern, system, or variation.

Let me share a few examples of my understanding with you. Let's take a flower. One flower might bloom alone, but it belongs to a species with genetic diversity.

Children may be born from the same parents, yet each one is different. Even twins, labelled as identical, are never truly the same. We are diverse. Everything around us reflects that diversity. There was not one mold used to shape everyone. There was a unique design for each of us. That is why the Divine Source is so vast, so layered, and so beautifully complex.

My truth is every person is a variation of the divine design—never repeated, never random. Now, this is making you unique. This is making you "one". But, even the "one" is still part of many. Therefore, nothing is truly alone. Diversity is not just around us. It is within us.

The Sacred Law of Diversity

I therefore define the Sacred Law of Diversity as the universal principle that reveals every creation is uniquely made and never repeated. It is the expression of Divine Intelligence through infinite variations—within us and all around us. Therefore, all creations are worthy of respect, love, and harmony, as they follow the sacred rhythm that leads them back into union with the Creator.

When we begin to see diversity—in people, beliefs, appearances, and expressions—with the same reverence we give to the seasons, the stars, or the oceans... Then we can begin to heal the division between us.

Just as we accept that there are different flowers, animals, climates, and sounds—we must accept that there are different people, with different complexities, intentions, languages, and truths. We are all born from the same Source—just expressed through infinite creative forms.

Because I am on this journey of self-discovery, I have learned to honor myself—my need, my boundaries and my truth. What truly makes me happy is what brings me peace. I am aware of the external noise, yet I cherish the quiet time I spend with myself, because I have discovered that everything meaningful is born from a place of love; and—that includes both me, and you.

So, as we begin to see diversity not as a challenge, but as a reflection of Divine Intelligence, we can expect a shift in the way we see one another. We can stop asking "Why are we so different?" and start wondering "What beauty can I find in your uniqueness?"

Because the questions we often asked ourselves introduce and shape the relationship we seek to build with the unseen. Each question and reflection opens a deeper part of ourselves—one that can stir fear and resentment or awaken openness and love. Every inner question is a seed that expands your vision of yourself, others, and humanity.

Therefore, do not take lightly the simple questions that arise in your mind, for the responses and beliefs you form around them shape not only your worldview but also the generational lens through which reality is perceived.

Have you ever silenced your uniqueness just to *belong*—because it felt almost wrong to simply *be yourself*? There are unseen forces that feed on our divisions and egos. The further we drift from ourselves, the further we move from our true essence.

It is not our variety that harms us—it is the fear, the ego, the conditioning that teaches us to separate, to rank, to reject. But when we embrace differences and diversity as sacred, we return to our natural state—one of unity, compassion, and spiritual awareness.

This is not about tolerance. This is not about fitting in. This is about remembering that *we were never meant to look the same, speak the same, or worship the same.* Diversity is not our flaw. It is our signature. It is the way the sacred reveals its complexity. To honor differences, is to recognize the fingerprints of the divine in every form.

When Sun fell in love with Water

Once upon a time, two opposites found love. The Sun fell in love with the Water.

The Sun was bold, radiant, full of fire and light. The Water was deep, reflective, soft and ever flowing. Though they were different in nature, they

The Sacred Law of Diversity

found harmony in their union. The Sun would shine, and the Water would reflect.

For a long time, the people of Earth wore only the colors of soil, stone, bark, and sand. Their world was painted in earth tones—practical, familiar, and muted. But the Sun and Water saw this and longed to gift something to Earth.

From their sacred union were born seven children—each a color, each a frequency, each a reflection of their love, and a different expression of light and depth. Red, Orange, Yellow, Green, Blue, Indigo, and Violet. Some were warm like their father. Others were cool like their mother. But each carried a piece of both.

Through them, the world came alive in diversity. Together, Sun and Water painted beauty for Earth. Flowers of every hue began to spring forth wherever Sun and Water danced—each bloom a reflection of their love and the imprint of their children. People began creating colorful clothing. Artists painted with new palettes. Children smiled wider. The fields blossomed.

Earth danced in harmony with this new melody, as the children of Sun and Water were not just colors. They were songs of creation, expressions of contrast. Each carrying a different emotion, a different gift, a different light.

Yet over time, the people of Earth began to forget. They no longer celebrated the variety of colors—they began to rank them, separate them, and declare some more beautiful or powerful than others.

The Sun grew quiet. The Water turned still.

But every now and then—when Earth needs to remember, she calls upon Wind to bring Water to Sun. And Sun, full of longing, leans down to kiss Water. And from that sacred kiss, all their children are shown beautifully together. Earth called it "Rainbow."

And every time she remembers that rainbow does not ask its colors to blend. It allows each one to shine.

It is a reminder written across the sky that all colors belong, and that beauty is not in uniformity, but in unity.

Each hue is holy, and when they stand side by side, the heavens open, and we remember: *Diversity is the signature of love.*

✦ ✦ ✦

This is not a political parable, nor a reference to any modern flag. It is a spiritual reflection on nature's own message: that opposites are not enemies, and diversity is not a flaw, but an expression of divine harmony. It honors the sacred design of difference.

This awareness brings us closer to the unseen, to others, and to ourselves. Many people seek to cultivate communication with the unseen without first balancing the ego and aligning with the understanding of nature. There are many voices. Recognizing who others are—and who you are—helps you navigate life with ears that hear beyond what is said and eyes that see beyond what is seen.

In the end, we are all individual rays of one light, and that light shines brighter when we allow each color to be seen. And for this to happen, we must look through the eyes of the spirit.

PART II

ALIGNMENT THROUGH THE EYES OF THE SPIRIT

Focus: inner healing, discernment, forgiveness, and spiritual alignment.

PISTIS: The Art of Trusting the Unseen

INTRODUCTION
Practices for Trusting the Unseen

I was recently watching a video that left me with a strange discomfort. "How in the world can someone think like that?" I wondered. Soon I realized I was caught in inner dialogues fueled by hate, ego, fear, and resentment. In that moment, the lesson became clear that I must learn to balance my inner world, to recognize which voices to quiet, and which one to trust and follow.

Life constantly tries to shape our inner world. That is why seeing through the lens of the soul becomes important. It helps us navigate life by learning which voice deserves our attention, and which one to stop feeding. For whatever voice we choose to nourish is the one that will guide us.

Some people may call this self-programming. Just as you install applications on your phone or computer, choosing which programs to use, so too, you can choose the conditions you allow into your inner life.

As we have seen in Part I, the unseen is a part of us, of everything and everyone around us. Therefore, to cultivate the *art of trusting the unseen* is to strengthen this *invisible* relationship with awareness, intention, and faith.

This second part of the book is about that relationship. It invites us into an awareness that can lighten the weight of life by consciously choosing thoughts, understandings, and actions that align with peace. My own self-programming, which helps me balance my *negative* and *positive* sides, has been to explore the divine mirror, forgiveness, the sacred yes, the language of dreams, the power of words, and manifestation guided by the soul. These are what I now share with you in each chapter.

As the world is filled with noise, without spiritual awareness, we often risk being carried by external voices. But when we see through the eyes of the soul, we rediscover freedom, clarity, and trust that naturally arises from within.

CHAPTER 8

THE DIVINE MIRROR

I used to go to church with my mother on Saturdays. When I was in my early teens, she transitioned from Catholicism to the Seventh-day Adventist faith, and so the Sabbath meant rising early, dressing neatly, and preparing not just her body—but her heart—for worship.

My mother often shared stories about her own childhood and the kind of church she knew growing up. She had gone to a Catholic school where the majority of the mass was in Latin. She would say, with a touch of irony, "Most of us Haitians did not even speak French—so imagine sitting through an hour-long sermon in Latin." And yet, Sunday after Sunday, people would show up, she explained. They would sit through sermons they could not understand, their faces solemn, their bodies present, but their minds wandering in the mystery of sounds that held no meaning to them.

"They came because it was good to come," she said. "Because it showed loyalty. Because it was what you do."

Even then, as a child, my mom had questions. She wondered why church was on Sunday when the Bible spoke of the Sabbath. She asked why we were taught that Jesus was born in December when so much pointed to something different.

"Every time I read something and understand it differently—yet see my community doing something else—I feel like we are all sitting and listening to a language we do not understand, but are still expected to follow. I cannot follow blindly," she would say.

Somehow, we always find a way to have conversations about life and religion. She never imposed any religion on us. She often reminded us that no religion can save, but only God. So, we all understood why she chose to transition to a Saturday church.

Now, looking back, I realize I may have inherited her curiosity—that relentless need to question, to understand, to see beyond what we are told. For a long time, I did not understand why *questioning* was important to her, until I started doing it myself.

Her church was only a five-minute walk from our neighborhood, just a few streets away. It became a new construction, built with the hands and hopes of the very people who worshipped inside it. Everyone had given something to make it rise from the ground: money, cement, nails, labor, prayers, etc.

When we go to church together, we would often pass familiar faces: the woman who sold produce at the corner, or the older man who sat outside under the mango tree... Most of them were also churchgoers, and most of them knew each other.

Even when I was not with my mother, walking home from school or just wandering through the neighborhood, strangers would greet me by my name and say things like, "Tell your mother I said hello." At first, it surprised me. I did not know them, but somehow, they knew me. It was a kind of invisible watchfulness, the community's way of keeping eyes on one another, making sure we were safe, seen, and staying out of trouble.

The Divine Mirror

One Saturday morning, I decided to go to church with my mother. The wooden pews were already half full, and a soft gospel melody lingered in the air like incense. My mom and I seated next to her "sisters in Christ," so they could worship together. They were women her age and older who would always greet me with warm smiles, ask how I was doing in school, and whether I had experienced any sickle cell episodes lately.

"We keep you in our prayers so you will no longer be sick." They would often say. It became easy to guess that my mother's main prayer for me was that I would stop suffering.

The preacher, a man with a warm presence and a voice that carried both strength and gentleness, stepped up to the pulpit. He opened his Bible slowly, as though holding something sacred and fragile at once. Then he said, "Today, we will talk about one of the most difficult commandments in scripture: *'Love your neighbor as yourself.'*" He paused, scanning the room.

I watched as heads nodded in familiarity. We all knew the phrase. We had heard it before. But somehow, the way he said it that day landed differently.

He went on, "Some days, I do not even like myself—so how could I love someone else with the same measure I cannot even offer inward?" His honesty surprised me, though I could not fully understand why. *Loving others as ourselves is what we are supposed to do as Christians,* I thought. Yet here was the pastor, openly admitting how difficult this could be.

At that time, if you had asked me why we should love like that, I would have answered, "*Because that is what the Bible says. That is what Jesus said. That is what God said.*" It was a mechanical response—one that did not require any deeper reflection on my part. I loved because I was told to love. But love, back then, did not carry much personal meaning. To me, it mostly meant *not hurting others*, because I did not want to be hurt myself. It felt more like a transaction than a transformation—but I was fine with that. We all were. We do not hurt, so we will not be hurt. We love, so we will be loved by God. Amen!

As the preacher continued, I allowed myself for the first time to go deeply into the verse and to read it inwardly, in a way that made sense to me. I realized that this verse was not only about "loving" *others*. It was also about the wounds we carry—the old pain buried beneath polished smiles—as we so often try to give what we have not yet truly received from ourselves. It was about the measure we use to love ourselves. It was not "loving" in exchange for salvation, but rather about offering a mirror of how we see and treat the world.

I began to understand that every book is someone's limited interpretation of the world. There were times in history when laws and rules did not truly exist, and in order for a command to be respected, it was easier to declare it divine so people would obey without question.

I started to wonder: why has the Black community often been the least loved around the world? And why did a religion that speaks so deeply of love, like Christianity, accept and even encourage slavery for centuries? Reflecting on my history and the beliefs I was raised with, I could not find a genuine answer that aligned with the true energy of love.

Somehow, that morning, this scripture opened something within me. Today, I understand it through a spiritual lens that I would like to share

The Divine Mirror

with you.

When you gaze into a mirror, you expect to see your face. You expect to see your features, your expression, perhaps even your flaws and beauty.

Have you ever imagined how many people around the world are doing the same thing? Looking into their mirror—big or small—to see what you see: a human form. Different faces, different lives, but the same act.

Some are looking into the mirror, hoping to see an image they cherish in their mind. Others will look with a smile, while some gaze with the memory of their younger self. But can the mirror truly show our whole truth?

Some of us look, yet still hope to be someone else. Someone we can love better. Someone who—perhaps because of different physical features—might be more accepted, more desired.

When you look into your mirror, what do you see? Do not just look at the physical. Look into your eyes for a moment and ask yourself: *What am I really seeing?*

Perhaps you are still your past. One look and you are pulled back into your struggles, your joy, your memories. Perhaps you are your present. One look and you are fully there—feet on the ground—contemplating the person you are today. Or maybe you are your future. You cannot yet see the person in front of you because you are projecting an image of someone who does not exist yet.

And still, your reflection remains—quietly showing you what only you can truly see.

So, seeing is not only about what we perceive with the eyes. Seeing is connected to the stories we cherish, and the ones we do not speak of. It is connected to the unseen and the untold. Behind every reflection, there is always something deeper—a soul that breathes, a spirit that wonders, a person trying to make sense of who they are.

Are we really that different?

Some of us are struggling to see ourselves in our own mirror because of lies we have been taught:

Lies about beauty standards.

Lies about who belongs and who does not.

Lies that make us blind to our own image.

Lies that make it hard to love the reflection we are seeing.

Because—just maybe—if we could be a little more like *them*, we think we would look better, be loved better, and therefore love better. But that, too, is an illusion—rooted in a mirage, showing something that seems true, desirable, or attainable, but when you get closer, it vanishes...

And so, with the same critical eyes we use to judge ourselves, we begin to look at others. A cycle begins. We pass those same fears and patterns on to the next generation. More criticism is formed. More approval is needed just to feel whole.

We lose the ability to love ourselves by listening to our own inner voice. In fact, we shut it down because we only trust the validations that come from outside of us. And without even realizing it, we become addicted. Addicted to an image of ourselves that others find lovable.

Without that approval, suddenly, we are nothing but the hollow echo of ourselves, standing in front of a mirror...

✦ ✦ ✦

In *Pistis*, which means *faith* or *trust*, it is impossible to speak of trusting the unseen without recognizing the foundation of that trust. Love is

The Divine Mirror

therefore the heart of all true spirituality. Strip away the doctrines, the rituals, the names we give to God, and what remains, if the path is genuine, is love. Not the fleeting emotion, but the enduring force that unites all creation.

To speak of the unseen without speaking of love would be incomplete because the unseen is not only mystery, but also intimacy. It is the part of the Divine, of ourselves, and of others that cannot be measured or proven, but only felt and known through the "heart," therefore, love is the language of that knowing.

Now, when you look at yourself in the mirror and your inner voice whispers, "I love myself," what are you truly saying? Perhaps, you are saying that you love the reflection you are seeing. Or, perhaps, you are saying that you also love the stories it holds.

So when you choose to love others, are you only loving the physical? Or are you also loving the unseen part—the one you cannot see but is just as real?

Imagine—just imagine that you went to a nice restaurant for dinner with friends. The food was so good that you asked for a small portion to take home. The next day, you warm up your food and, with the first spoonful, you close your eyes and smile. The food was good yesterday, and it is just as good today. But was there any magic? Any hidden formula behind why it still tastes so good?

When you open your eyes and look at your spoon, you realize something simpler: the container you put it in may be different—a box, a bowl, a foil wrap—but the meal is the same. The flavor is still there. The ingredients have not changed, and that is the only reason you are tasting the same food you enjoyed the day before.

The secret is never in the container, but in the ingredients—blended and melted into one another—that make it flavorful. The container is just a design, a presentation, a disposable tool. You would not buy a dish solely because it comes in a beautiful container; you would choose it for its taste. And often, the most flavorful ingredients are the ones you no longer see once the dish is complete.

That is how I see us as people. Different containers. Different looks. Some taller, some darker, some louder. But what we carry inside are ingredients made from the same recipe. Some may add a little more spice, some may cook it longer, some may even forget the salt—but the essence is still the same.

So when you look at someone, do not stop at the container. Because when you look in your own mirror, you already know there is more to you than your human form.

Just like you are a blend of the seen and the unseen, try to see others as a complete recipe—one that life has seasoned differently—not just as a container.

The *perfection* we often expect others to conform to is nothing more than the chains in our own hands—chains we cannot see—that keep us enslaved to ideologies and thoughts dancing in our mind like shadows at midday.

The *Divine Mirror* is inviting us to see ourselves first and truly—not out of judgment, but out of understanding.

The *Divine Mirror* never stops at the physical. If you stand in front of a mirror long enough, you begin speaking to a part of yourself that is rarely revealed to others. A part that is often vulnerable. So vulnerable that some of us close our eyes or turn our heads—as if we are not yet ready to truly see ourselves.

It is a silent invitation to see beyond what your eyes can perceive. To release the need to control, even of your own reflection. To pause. To witness. To truly see yourself. To take a moment to truly see others; because you can.

By seeing yourself, you learn to see others. This is the *Divine Mirror*. This is how you learn to love others as yourself.

✦ ✦ ✦

Love comes from understanding, not just of others, but of ourselves. The kind of understanding that does not divide, compare or shrink, but includes everyone in our sense of truth.

I offer you this: *We love, when we remember who we are.*

Most of what the world calls love is conditional. It is based on how people treat us, what they give, how well they fit into our beliefs. But spiritual love—the love that heals, transforms and elevates, begins with one essential awareness: *We are all connected.*

Scientists have observed that when sound is produced near water, the liquid responds by shifting, vibrating, and forming intricate patterns that mirror the shape and frequency of the sound itself. This reveals that sound is not formless; it carries structure, intention, and the power to shape the physical world. When it finds a medium, like water or matter, to reveal its hidden form. This means sound is not merely something we hear. It is something that creates. It produces form. It holds codes. It expresses the unseen into the seen.

This reflects both the scientific and spiritual

understanding of the essence of life. From the Big Bang, believed to be the first "sound" of creation, to the primordial "Om" in Hinduism, and the "In the beginning was the Word" in Christian scripture—all suggest that creation began not with form, but with *vibration*. With *sound.*

To me, this illustrates that *we are all connected* by the same invisible thread—a vibration so deep, so pure that resonates within the fabric of consciousness itself. And to me, the closest replica of this Divine vibration is *love*. Love is a frequency that can awaken something unexplainable within us. It often comes like a presence that can clarify the voice of our inner knowing. It is in love that we often hear the loudest "yes" or the most necessary "no." Whether we identify as spiritual, mystical, or neither—when we love, we feel more connected to our inner self than ever before.

At the heart of "we are all connected" is the understanding that all beings: humans, animals, nature, and even the unseen, are threads woven into the same energy. Our thoughts, emotions, and actions ripple outward and affect others, even when we are not aware of it. Spiritually, this means we are not isolated bodies, but vibrating fields of consciousness connected by unseen threads. When we hurt someone, we hurt ourselves. When we love someone, we heal a part of ourselves.

Thus, love is no longer a transaction made in hopes of salvation, but an awakening to the unseen web that connects us all through consciousness. Like roots beneath the earth, our actions, individual and collective, intertwine across generations. Some nations have made decisions in the past to take from other countries—only to realize, years later, that those actions would have consequences on their own internal structures. The

The Divine Mirror

unseen laws of balance do not bend simply because we fail to remember who we are.

Creation is not blind. It moves in cycles: transformation, collapse, rebirth. Over and over, until we finally turn inward and see the center of the circle. The Source. The thread. The truth that what we do to others, we do to ourselves.

"Loving others as ourselves" becomes this kind of love that grows from compassion and of the recognition that I am walking through my own sacred lessons, shaped by patterns, wounds and transformations, and so is everyone else.

Their lessons are not better or worse—just different. And whether we understand their behavior or not, whether we agree or not—it is all part of a journey greater than our understanding.

If we are still seeing others only through their skin, their status, or their similarity to us—we are not yet ready to love them; and we may not yet be truly loving ourselves.

Carl Jung once said: *"Everything that irritates us about others can lead us to an understanding of ourselves."* Love others not because they are easy to love, but because you have begun to understand the meaning of existence.

Love does not always mean closeness. Sometimes, the most loving act is to create distance with clarity, not resentment. Distance can give both souls the space they need to realign with their own path. Some connections are meant to be temporary. Honoring your boundaries is not a rejection of love; it is an expression of harmony with your true Self, and a way of cultivating self-respect and inner peace.

Spiritual love is not about tolerating harm or forcing connection. It is about seeing the divine in another while still listening to your own soul's guidance.

When someone is no longer meant to walk with you, your inner compass will whisper that truth. Listen. Their departure does not require anger or hate. You can release them with compassion. Love, in its highest form, brings peace, even from a distance.

True love is not only reflection, but recognition. The recognition that the same divine breath flows through every soul.

The African Ubuntu philosophy teaches: *"I am because we are."* Therefore, to harm another is to harm yourself. To love another is to affirm your own humanity.

As we are learning about ourselves, it becomes easier to love others as extensions of ourselves. Across faiths and philosophies, this message continues:

> *"The second is this: 'Love your neighbor as yourself.' There is no commandment greater than these."*
> —Mark 12:31 (NIV)

> *"Regard your neighbor's gain as your own gain, and your neighbor's loss as your own loss."*
> —T'ai Shang Kan Ying Pien

> *"This is the sum of duty: do not do to others what would cause pain if done to you."*
> —Mahabharata 5:1517

> *"See the brotherhood of all mankind as the highest order of Yogis; conquer your own mind, and conquer the world."*
> —Guru Nanak

> *"None of you truly believes until he wishes for his*

The Divine Mirror

brother what he wishes for himself."
—Hadith (Prophet Muhammad, peace be upon him)

"[...] That which is hateful to you, do not do to another; that is the entire Torah; and the rest is its interpretation."
— Talmud, Shabbat 31a

Many spiritual teachings speak of seeing ourselves in others, but true spiritual love goes beyond recognition as it becomes action.

It invites us to offer the same patience, kindness, care, and forgiveness to others that we would want for ourselves. Not because they are perfect. But because they are us—in a different body, on a different path, carrying the same divine breath.

In *Pistis*, this understanding becomes even more meaningful. Trusting the unseen includes *seeing the unseen in others*—their stories, their path, their divine design. It begins by trusting the unseen within yourself first; because how you love yourself sets the tone for how you love the world.

If you are struggling to feel love for someone who has caused you pain, close your eyes and repeat: "We are all connected, and I am simply learning. Thank you for being an instrument helping my understanding." Now, picture them as a child: open, vulnerable and still learning. Now, take a deep breath and repeat: "You are on your path. I release you with peace."

This is love—not control, not judgement, but the recognition of the sacred lessons that you have shared and the understanding that it may be time for your journeys to continue in different directions.

Always remember; just as someone can be an

instrument of pain in your life, you too—consciously or unconsciously—may have been an instrument of pain in someone else's.

We are all connected. We are all learning from one another. And sometimes, the deepest learning comes from the hardest encounters; the ones that ask us to remember love even when it hurts. This is where forgiveness begins in remembering who we are beyond the pain.

CHAPTER 9

THE PRINCIPLE OF FORGIVENESS

Before the word "forgiveness" was ever spoken, it was a vibration—a frequency within the divine mind, echoing across the unseen realms. Today, we try to define it in human terms: the conscious decision to release resentment, to let go of the weight caused by another's action or our own.

From psychological healing to religious doctrine, forgiveness is praised as a virtue—a choice that sets the forgiver free more than the forgiven. Yet beyond these definitions lies something deeper: forgiveness is not just a moral decision—it is an act of spiritual liberation. It is a return to wholeness.

In many traditions, to forgive means "to give before." To offer grace before justice, love before understanding. This is not seen as weakness, but a sacred power. It is the ability to rise beyond our pain, beyond our ego, and remember that we are not just wounded beings but divine souls in human form.

Many Indigenous spiritualities view forgiveness as returning to balance—not only for the individual but for the entire community and for the spiritual world.

For example, in Navajo spirituality, life is meant

to be lived in *Hózhó*—a state of balance, beauty, harmony, and right relationship with the self, others, nature, and the spiritual realms. When someone commits a harmful act—through anger, dishonesty, or violence—they are said to be "*out of Hózhó*." This disturbance is not seen only as an individual issue; it ripples through the family, the tribe, and even the spirit world.

To restore balance, ceremonial practices like the *Enemy Way* are performed. These are not intended to punish, but to heal, to restore harmony between all affected, including ancestors, the land, and the unseen forces that support life. The goal is not to shame the one who erred, but to guide them back to harmony and spiritual alignment.

Buddhism teaches that holding onto anger is like grasping a hot coal with the intent of throwing it at someone else—in the end, you are the one who gets burned.

Metta (loving-kindness) meditation includes forgiving oneself and others as a way to dissolve resentment and create inner freedom.

As we enter this chapter, I invite you to gently remove the armor you have worn to survive; not to forget the wounds, but to look at them with new eyes. Forgiveness is not about denying your story—it is about rewriting its meaning through the lens of the soul.

Just like love, forgiveness requires understanding. Not intellectual understanding, but a deeper, soul-level knowing—one that sees beyond the actions, beyond the words, and into the sacred journey of others.

We each walk a different path. Though we may

cross, intertwine, or even collide with others, our soul's mission is uniquely designed. When someone hurts you, it is easy to only see the wound. But if you pause and look beyond the pain, you may begin to see a soul who is still learning, just as you are. A soul who, perhaps unknowingly, is acting from their own unhealed places.

This does not excuse harm, but it helps us see behavior without attaching it to someone's identity. They are not the harm. They are a being on the path, navigating life with a level of awareness that may be different from yours.

Forgiveness is the result of this spiritual seeing. It is the heart's way of saying: "I understand that we have different lessons. We do not carry the same awareness, and our souls' compass is different. And that's okay. I release you from my judgment, and I release myself from the bondage of pain."

I often speak of "path" and "mission" because this recognition—that we are all here fulfilling different soul contracts—transforms how we see people and events.

Suddenly, betrayal becomes a teacher. Disappointment becomes a mirror. Even cruelty becomes a contrast that strengthens our own commitment to compassion. We no longer ask, "Why did they do this to me?" but rather, "What is my soul being invited to understand here?"

When you begin to view others through the lens of their own unfolding journey, the grip of resentment loosens, and in its place, you find something unexpected—peace.

> *"Forgive them, for they do not know what they are doing."*
> —Luke 23:34 (NIV)

Spoken by Jesus while on the cross, this shows forgiveness as a divine act of mercy, even in the face of deep injustice; he understood that they did not know what they were doing.

From my spiritual understanding, forgiveness is more than "releasing for our own good"—it is "releasing because we understood."

It is not just about lightening our emotional load or finding peace of mind. It is deeper than self-preservation. True forgiveness is releasing because we have seen the truth behind the veil. We have understood the imperfection of the moment, the limits of our awareness, the karmic patterns at play, and the fact that we are all walking a path of remembering.

Forgiveness becomes not an escape, but a sacred conclusion—the soul's way of saying, "Now that I see the whole picture, I no longer need to hold this pain."

This kind of forgiveness does not rush. It comes when understanding ripens in the heart. When we stop seeing people through the lens of what they did and start seeing them as who they are becoming. When we realize that we have also been the one who hurt, the one who did not know better, the one who failed to show up with love—and someone, somewhere, chose to release us too. That is when forgiveness is no longer an act of emotional hygiene, but a soul alignment.

It becomes a reminder that we are all in process, and that pain is often the side effect of growth not yet completed.

We often think that by holding onto our pain, we are protecting ourselves. But in truth, we are paying for that pain daily—with our peace, our energy, and our joy. Resentment becomes a silent tax on the soul. The longer we carry it, the heavier

The Principle of Forgiveness

it grows in our minds and in our bodies. Some wounds need time. But others remain open because we keep pressing on them with thoughts, memories, and stories that no longer serve us.

And then, there is the most difficult act of all: *forgiving ourselves.* For the things we did. For the things we allowed. For not knowing better. For not being stronger. But self-forgiveness is not earned through punishment, it is offered through compassion. When you understand that your past self was doing the best it could with what it knew, a softening happens. And in that softening, healing begins.

My truth is that we are all capable of doing what we call good or bad, right or wrong. These qualities do not belong to some people and not others—they live in all of us. They are not fixed traits—they are choices.

As explained in chapter 4, we are spiritual beings in a human experience, we carry both light and shadow. What makes the difference is the lessons we have already learned and the choices we now make.

A person who chooses not to harm is not "better" than someone who does—they are simply walking on a different part of the journey. Perhaps they have already been through the pain of harming or being harmed in a past they cannot remember. Perhaps their spirit now says: "I know this road, and I no longer want to walk it."

A relationship with the unseen is, ultimately, a relationship with yourself. Trust is built when you can see both your flaws and your beauty, and choose to walk with yourself fully and honestly.

✦ ✦ ✦

PISTIS: The Art of Trusting the Unseen

I remember one Christmas; my little niece came to visit. She was only three at the time—curious, innocent, and full of wonder. In the living room, I had a small, scented lamp with warm wax that melts from the heat of a bulb to release a beautiful fragrance. We told her precisely, again and again, "Do not touch—it's hot, it will burn you." But as children do, she waited until no one was watching and dipped her tiny finger into the wax.

She cried instantly—not because anyone punished her, but because the heat hurt. Thankfully, it was just wax, and the pain passed quickly. But something changed. From that day on, whenever I went to turn it off, she was the one warning me to be careful. She remembered.

That is exactly how the spirit remembers and warns us.

Have you ever felt tempted to do something and suddenly, a voice within whispers no? It is not fear. It is not guilt. It is memory.

Forgiveness becomes easier when you understand this. People are learning. Just like that child, they may not know the fire burns until they touch it themselves. And after they do, they will remember. That memory allows them to make choices based on their current path and lessons.

In spirituality, it is also said that before we are born, we choose our parents, our name, date of birth, our environment, and even the challenges we will face. Not from a place of punishment, but as a divine preparation for the lessons our soul needs in this lifetime.

"But the angel said to her, "Do not be afraid, Mary;

The Principle of Forgiveness

you have found favor with God. You will conceive and give birth to a son, and you are to call him Jesus. He will be great and will be called the Son of the Most High."
—Luke 1:30–32 (NIV)

The story of a divine child born of light is not confined to one name, one land, or one faith. The names like Horus, Krishna, Buddha, Mithra, Zoroaster and Jesus speak through humanity's memory. Across time and tradition, we find the recurring arrival of the One who comes through mystery to heal, to teach and to remind us of who we truly are.

Let me take the story of Jesus as example, for it reflects a spiritual pattern found in many beliefs. His birth was not accidental. His parents were chosen; his mission was known before his arrival. He was sent, not simply born. His incarnation was not random but shaped for a divine purpose.

This supports the idea that we, too, come with a specific purpose and choose the vessel through which we enter this world.

Every soul carries a blueprint. Within it, certain experiences are chosen not only for our highest good, but for the highest good of all those we encounter. The family we enter, the land we are born into, the body we inhabit—none of it is random. These are sacred agreements, made in realms of light, where the soul says: "This time, I want to learn patience." Or, "This time, I want to remember how to love myself after betrayal." And so, we are born into the perfect soil for that remembering.

When we see life through this lens, even our most painful relationships take on a different meaning. Forgiveness becomes less about letting go of what someone did, and more about honoring the divine contract that helped us grow.

Every day, we make choices shaped by who we have been, who we are now, and who we are becoming. Sometimes, we do things that do not feel aligned with our true self. And even if no one else notices, we can feel it deeply. That's the spirit remembering. The soul knows when something goes against its growth.

So, when we choose not to act in harmful ways, it's not because we are perfect. It's because something within us has already learned that lesson. And when someone else makes a choice that we would not, it doesn't mean they are flawed, it means they are still learning.

This understanding changes everything. It reminds us that we are all capable of anything—and that what matters is the direction we choose now. From that place, forgiveness can grow. Not from judgment, but from compassion. Because when we recognize that others are also souls in progress, we stop needing to label them. Instead, we simply understand.

From my spiritual understanding, this may be why—when the Europeans arrived on the island once called Quisqueya in 1492, later named Hispaniola by the Spaniards, and now known as Haiti (from the Taíno word Ayiti, meaning "land of high mountains") and the Dominican Republic—the Taíno people, who inhabited the island, welcomed them, even though they had likely never seen anyone who looked like them before. It was not ignorance. It was not weakness. It reflected their spiritual worldview and understanding at this time.

The people of Quisqueya had a sacred way of seeing life. To them, human beings were more than bodies or skin color. They understood that life was cyclical, that every encounter held meaning, and that each soul belonged to the earth, the stars, and the spirit world.

Even though they were later labeled "savages" and their ceremonies dismissed as "pagan," they lived in alignment with the land, the elements, and ancestral wisdom. Their view of humanity was far more holistic than the narrow lens through which colonial Christianity viewed the world.

The Europeans arrived with a different kind of knowledge—one rooted in conquest, hierarchy, and fear of the unknown. They worshipped one God and followed Christianity, while the people of Quisqueya were accused of worshipping false gods. Yet despite their opposing beliefs, both were linked to a spiritual path. Their encounter—though marked by violence and misunderstanding—was part of a higher, transformative journey. From a spiritual perspective, both people were participating in a greater unfolding. They were not meeting solely for conflict, but to ignite a shift in human consciousness. As painful as that meeting was, it carried the seeds of awakening, for both the colonizers and the colonized.

I am here today—a daughter of Ayiti, writing this book—I am a living result of that transformation.

In this light, forgiveness for these historical wounds is not about forgetting or excusing the violence. It is about understanding the deeper movements of spirit across time—how souls, nations, and histories all participate in a greater unfolding.

Some of the wounds we carry do not belong to us alone. They are carried through bloodlines—passed from those who came before us, still present in our thoughts, fears, and dreams. To forgive is also to release generations from a pattern. It is to say: *"This pain ends with me."* Because to trust the unseen, is to work on all parts of ourselves that still carries hurt, pain, and fear.

I read this verse many times, but now truly understand its meaning:

> *"[...] If anyone slaps you on the right cheek, turn to them the other cheek also."*
> —Matthew 5:39 (NIV)

It reflects a radical form of compassion, not rooted in weakness, but in spiritual strength and understanding.

Some may think you are naïve to forgive, but you are not. You have simply moved beyond that lesson.

I forgive because I understand who I am now and because I understand others too, without needing to change them or direct their path. I do not forgive and hold on; I forgive and truly let go.

The indifference one might feel after I choose to forgive can sometimes seem hurtful. Because when the pain is no longer there to hold anything between us, there is no reaction, no anger, no confrontation. Some people expect you to yell, to curse or act out. But, when true understanding has taken place, and the lesson has been fully integrated, only silence remains. There is no need to resist the circumstances because the soul has already received what it needed to learn, and peace has already spoken.

Therefore, to forgive is to loosen the soul from its own chains. But true release does not come only from letting go of others—it comes from remembering the Self beneath the story. That Self was never broken as it was just learning...

CHAPTER 10

LISTENING FOR THE SACRED YES

Earlier in this book, I spoke about the *divine invitation*—the soul's choice to incarnate, to grow, to remember. But recognizing that invitation when it appears in real life, often disguised as a difficult decision, a new path, or even a closed door is not always easy.

That is where the Sacred Yes comes in. It is the part of the journey where the soul speaks back, and if we are quiet enough to listen, we will hear it saying: *This is yours.*

The Sacred Yes is not just a good feeling or a lucky opportunity; it is a deep inner knowing, a spiritual confirmation. It does not always feel exciting or obvious. Sometimes it feels humbling, silent, or uncomfortable, but it resonates with truth and alignment.

Unlike the "ego yes"—decisions driven by fear, pressure, or the need to please—the Sacred Yes is rooted in peace. It may not be loud, but it is always clear.

The ego says yes is often to what is loud, urgent, and externally rewarded. While the soul says yes to what is still, lasting and inwardly confirmed.

The Sacred Yes does not always arrive in the

same form. It can speak through your inner voice, a stranger's word, a song that stirs your soul unexpectedly, or even a dream. It is your spirit, finding a way to reach you.

I used to write a lot as a teenager. Any of my childhood friends and close family members can testify to this. I wrote so much that my middle finger is now slightly deformed from how long I used to hold my pen. I was always inspired and filled notebooks, journals, and even homemade booklets that I stapled together and shared with classmates. Writing, from an early age, became my way of keeping track of my conversations with the unseen.

When I was in law school, some of my professors pointed out how difficult it was to read my legal assignments.

I remember during my first year, for a public law assessment, I began my introduction with a quote from Victor Hugo and spent the first part of my paper exploring his ideas, along with those of other authors like Descartes and Machiavelli. For me, it was a way to create a parallel of thoughts before addressing the core issue of the question that was asked.

The result? A D minus.

I was surprised. Usually, my writing worked. But somehow, I just could not find my balance.

Legal writing, they explained: required a specific structure. It must be direct, precise, and argumentative, which was very different from the poetic style I naturally used.

For me, a simple question was always more than just "rules and laws." It was about understanding, introspection—what could be learned, appreciated, and reformed. But in law, there was no time for philosophy.

I had learned that if I want to win, I must be direct. I could cite one article, and the case could be dismissed in favor of my client. As a lawyer, I was not a lawmaker. That kind of discussion belongs in the parlement, not in the courtroom.

At the time, I could not understand my way of thinking. I remember freezing when I was asked a question—not necessarily because I did not understand, but because I was afraid of saying more than I was supposed to. And when I was writing, there were always too many sentences, too many ideologies, too many thoughts.

I did not want to simply repeat the law; I wanted to reform it, to review it, to amend it.

I loved analyzing everything I read, so I could find more than what was asked. And in doing so—I was failing... I had to learn to put aside my inner voice in order to write like a lawyer.

By my third year, I had mastered it. The university sent me for a public law internship at the Senate of the country, where I wrote a bill and was later awarded by the Junior Chamber International, in partnership with the Canadian Embassy in Haiti, as a national winner in Governmental, Judicial, and Political Affairs. I even presented my final legal thesis—focused on the importance of clarity and accessibility in lawmaking, and how to write laws in a way that people can truly understand—to earn my law degree.

At that time, I thought I was on a strong, secure path. I did not feel particularly guided, I was motivated by survival. I wanted a stable future, a profession, a way to take care of myself and support my family. Isn't that true for many of us?

Somewhere along the way, I forgot if I was ever guided at all.

I forgot the little booklets I once made out of

paper, glued together and filled with my own handwritten stories. I even overlooked the fact that my very first full-time job was writing for a newspaper.

Now, in the middle of my second year working as a litigation paralegal at a national law firm in the U.S, my inner voice whispered again: *"It is time."*

"But if I leave" I responded, "how will I pay my bills? What about my apartment, my car, my insurance?"

The Sacred Yes does not always make sense. But it always brings alignment. Sometimes, something simply feels right—even if you can't fully explain it. It brings peace. It opens space in your spirit.

Still, I resisted. I was unsure. I was afraid; but then, life started speaking louder.

I wanted to make sure that what I was hearing was not coming from a place of anger or uncertainty. Despite all the experiences I had, I was still doubting. Because truthfully, after structuring life solely around career and responsibilities, there's often no space left for the inner whisper to be heard.

I kept asking for clarity, again and again. Every time something did not make sense, I would ask: "What is this here to teach me? What am I being called to listen to?"

One morning, I woke up with a coworker on my mind. On the drive to work, I felt a clear message: *Buy her flowers.* It was a Friday—and I listened.

I was told by my inner compass that she was going through a transformation, and that my compassion would be helpful. The message was simple: *Let her know she is loved, and she will be fine.*

So, I bought the flowers. In the note, I wrote something similar to: You are loved, and you will be fine—whatever it is you are facing. On Tuesday

Listening for the Sacred Yes

or Wednesday of next week, she was gone. She was no longer with the company. We did not have the chance to see each other.

I was, in some way, glad that I had listened to my inner voice—the one that urged me to show compassion without knowing what would come of it. In that silence, my spirit whispered: "Here's your confirmation..."

But it also said this:

"You are not asking what you are here to learn from trust—you are asking through fear. You already know the truth. The answer is within you. Now, it is up to you to follow." And weeks later, other situations unfolded that gave me clarity...

✦ ✦ ✦

If you are unsure, ask for clarity—not from a place of fear, but from a place of deep introspection and willingness to understand.

You might ask: "But how do I know it is my Sacred Yes and not just emotion, fear, or excitement?"

The Sacred Yes is consistent. It stays with you, even in silence. It brings peace. It aligns with who you are becoming—not who you are trying to impress. It reminds you of who you are. It may not always make you comfortable, but it will make you more honest with yourself.

Sometimes, the Sacred Yes appears at the very same door where fear stands guard. We hesitate, not because we do not know what to do, but because the path ahead requires us to become someone we have not fully stepped into yet. Resistance often signals proximity to purpose.

I have learned that when you silence the Sacred Yes, life will eventually find a way to wake you up.

PISTIS: The Art of Trusting the Unseen

It may be through discomfort, through restlessness, or through a series of closed doors. Not as punishment, but as redirection. Ignoring the Yes does not remove your calling. It only delays your peace.

Once you say yes from the soul, you may notice how things begin to move. A conversation, or an opportunity... This is the dance of alignment. The Sacred Yes is not just internal—the *Universe* responds to it.

For a long time, I shaped my life according to what the world expected of me. I followed the steps—study hard, succeed, perform, survive. And I was good at it. I loved parts of it too. But in embracing that version of myself, the one who could perform, present, and deliver in the ways the world wanted, I unknowingly abandoned something precious. A part of myself that I had buried beneath responsibility. Something I thought could be kept as a hobby, a side project, maybe something I would return to "one day."

But my spirit had other plans. It whispered a truth I was not quite ready to hear—this is not just something you do. This is who you are.

The spiritual part of me was never absent, just buried. Waiting. My writing, too, was never lost. It lived quietly in my hands, in the way I saw the world, in the way I listened deeply to my own inner rhythm—even when I could not always explain it.

Now, it is my time to respond to my Sacred Yes.

Your spirit never forgets. It always knows who you truly are. Even when the world teaches you to become something else. Even when you drift far from your essence, your spirit waits—patiently—

Listening for the Sacred Yes

for the moment you will come back home.

That moment is the Sacred Yes.

It is the remembrance that you are not here to fit in—you are here to awaken. You are not here to perform—you are here to align. And you are not here to chase a title—you are here to live your truth.

> *"There is a voice that doesn't use words. Listen."*
> *"Let yourself be silently drawn by the strange pull of what you really love. It will not lead you astray."*
> —Rumi

It's also important to remember that not all Sacred Yes moments look the same. My Sacred Yes might lead me to walk away from something that, for you, would be a sacred beginning. What calls my soul may have nothing to do with what calls yours, and that is exactly how it's meant to be.

This is why knowing your mission—your soul's unique assignment—matters. Your Sacred Yes is not a trend, a formula, or a copy of someone else's success. It is your truth. It is a vibration, an alignment, a resonance that only your spirit can truly recognize.

When you try to follow someone else's path, you may reach their results, but miss your own purpose.

The spiritual path is not something you borrow. It rises from within. It is coded in your being. It will align with who you truly are, not who the world told you to become. And when you stop chasing external approval and turn inward to listen, you will realize that your path was always there, patiently waiting for your Yes.

> *"The drumbeat of the Earth knows your name. When*

you finally remember your rhythm, you will return to the path."
—paraphrased Indigenous teaching.

To further explain my thoughts, I will share the story of the lioness and the Sacred Yes. It is a reflection that came to me when I began asking: *what happens when the soul finally says yes?* Because it is not always a voice. Sometimes, it is the pull in your chest when you think of something that feels impossible but peaceful. It is the feeling of home before you arrive. A strange stillness that says: *Yes, this way.*

✦ ✦ ✦

The Story of the Lioness and the Sacred Yes
Once upon a time, there was a city of lions.
This city had pledged allegiance to a powerful king, and in return, he offered them their own land—with one condition: they would have everything they wanted, but they could never leave. Not only them, but every generation after would be required to perform in the royal circus.
Generations passed, and the lions were bathed, dressed, and trained to entertain. Performing for the palace became a mark of success. It was the path every lion was expected to follow—to be admired, celebrated, and loved.
New generations no longer remembered who they were. They chased after everything that shined, unaware of their true nature.
Among them was a lioness who had become one of the best performers. She smiled on command, danced when asked, and bowed before the crowd. But deep within, something stirred. She felt that she could run further. That her power was greater

than the cage allowed. She could roar louder, but was told to stay quiet, so the people would not be afraid.

The voice inside her would not leave. It said: *There is more. You are more.*

She tried to ignore it, but it stayed—year after year, show after show.

When she spoke to the others, some admitted they had felt the same thing before. But they had silenced it. The palace was comfortable. Predictable. Safe. Why would they want anything different? But she no longer wanted safety, she wanted truth.

And so, one day, during a grand performance, she stopped smiling. She stood tall, looked at the crowd, and roared with all the force in her spirit.

The people screamed. The circus emptied. She was tranquilized and placed in a cage. But to her, the cage was no different than the palace. She had always been imprisoned—limited from being her full self. So, she waited.

One night, when the guards had grown tired and careless, she escaped.

She ran with no map. She had no promise of safety. Only a whisper in her soul that said: *Go.*

For weeks, she wandered—hungry, tired, alone. But she kept running.

Then one day, she reached a vast, open land. A place she had never seen before. There, she could run without limits. Roar without fear. And when she roared again, this time—it echoed freely. Suddenly, from the distance, other lions appeared. They had been waiting too.

It was then she realized: The performance had been a beautiful prison she was taught to love. But her Sacred Yes had led her freely home.

PISTIS: The Art of Trusting the Unseen

The Sacred Yes is less about achievement and more about alignment. Less about arrival and more about remembrance.

The longer we ignore our Sacred Yes, the harder it becomes to recognize our own voice. Not because it disappears—but because our inner space becomes filled with everyone else's. We begin to question ourselves, delay our becoming, and settle into patterns that feel safe but slowly dim our light. Saying Yes is not about rushing, but the knowing that we no longer pretend that we cannot hear.

Tonight, before you sleep, place your hand over your heart and ask: *Is there a Yes I have silenced?* You do not need the full answer now. Just the willingness to ask is enough to begin again.

May you have the courage to say yes to your truth—even if your voice trembles, even if your path seems unclear—your soul knows the way. Saying yes to the unseen and the unknown is, ultimately, saying yes to yourself. There is no greater act of faith than that.

CHAPTER 11

DREAMS: CONVERSATIONS BETWEEN REALMS

Sometimes, the voice of the inner self arrives not in daylight, but in dreams. Not in words, but in symbols—and, this too, is the path.

I cannot give a proper definition of dreams—not yet. I know there are scientific explanations and spiritual interpretations, but for me, dreams remain a journey of discovery, and therefore are important in knowing who I am. They are not something I have mastered or fully understood. They are something I continue to experience, and each dream opens another door I did not know existed.

Some dreams feel like whispers from within. Others feel like messages from beyond. In this chapter, I explore both: the discovery of dream language, and the moments when dreams became undeniable truth.

✦ ✦ ✦

Dreams, to me, are portals—gateways to a vastness of possibility. Sometimes they feel blurred, uncertain, like trying to remember a song you heard a long time ago. At other times, they come in vivid, colorful landscapes that feel more real than waking life. That is why it always felt strange to see movies portraying dreams in black and white.

My dreams are almost always in color. And not just any color—sometimes, a particular shade will stand out, glowing with meaning. I do not always know why... but I notice it.

Try to keep a journal beside your bed this week. Each morning, write down anything you remember from your dreams: colors, feelings, or fragments. Don't worry if it's messy. Just notice. Then ask yourself:" How does your dream world feel different from your waking one? What is it inviting you to see?" Try to be more present each time. When you go to sleep, do it with the intention of discovery. As if you were setting out on an adventure with yourself. Know that you can be as conscious in your dreams as you are in your waking life.

> *"Natural transformation processes announce themselves mainly in dreams."*
> —Carl Jung (The Collected works of C.G. Jung, Vol9)

As a teenager in Haiti, long before I ever read anything about "lucid dreaming," I was already living it. I kept a journal by my bed and would write down my dreams, especially the ones that stayed with me long after waking.

Some made no sense at first—disconnected scenes or strange stories. But I remembered them, and that remembering made me curious.

Without knowing the terminology, I began experimenting. I challenged myself to return to a

Dreams: Conversations Between Realms

dream—to see if I could go back and explore it again. Sometimes it worked. Sometimes it didn't. But what fascinated me most was that even when I thought the dream had an "ending," it never really did. It just... moved. Shifted. Transformed. One scene led to another, and the journey continued.

Over time, I realized that I could learn in my dreams. If I had a difficult assignment or question in real life, I would try to bring the subject into the dream world. Sometimes, I would find answers—or at least, new ideas. Creative solutions. I would get writing inspiration or feel led to something I did not expect.

I also noticed that I could think in my dreams. And when I start thinking, I will realize that I was dreaming. That is what intrigues me most. I was aware of my thoughts—asking questions, receiving answers—as if in conversation with myself, or something deeper within. Sometimes I would find myself in frightening scenarios, and I would consciously try to change the dream. Sometimes it worked. Sometimes it did not. But I was present, and that presence changed everything.

It became a personal challenge: How far could I go in my dreams? Could I guide them? Could I reshape them? This was not about control, it was about understanding the power of thought, even in sleep.

There was a boy at school I liked, and I often tried to bring him into my dreams, just so I could see him again. I now know this is called lucid dreaming, but back then, it was just a secret world I explored by night.

> *"I often think that the night is more alive and more richly colored than the day."*
> —Vincent Van Gogh.

Later, during university, I continued my personal research and learned more about what scientists and spiritual teachers were saying about dreams. Still, even with all the theories, I never believed dreams were only subconscious thoughts. Some dreams hold too much wisdom, too much mystery.

After certain dreams, I don't just feel like I saw something—I feel like I became something new. I wake up knowing that we, as human beings, carry far more potential than we realize. That there are realms within us we have not even begun to understand. But not all dreams were just personal explorations. Some came with a purpose, and changed everything...

On the night of January 11, 2010, I was in pain. My left knee was swollen, and the ache kept me from sleeping. Late that evening, my father came into my room. He sat beside me and asked how I was doing. I told him about my knee, and with a gentle smile, he said: "I will kiss your knee, and the pain will go away."

He kissed my knee, then kissed my forehead, and wished me goodnight.

It would be the last time I ever saw him. I was twenty years old.

That night, I barely slept. The pain kept me awake for hours. It wasn't until around 7 a.m. on January 12 that I finally drifted off. What happened next would stay with me forever.

I dreamed that I was walking near my old high school. The road was strangely quiet—until, suddenly, a cloud of dust surrounded me. I looked around and saw houses and buildings collapsing. People were walking past me in larger numbers than usual, but their faces were covered in dust and streaked with blood. They were crying. Stumbling. Wounded.

I thought: Was there an explosion?

I stood still in the middle of the road, watching the chaos.

Then, out of nowhere, a woman dressed entirely in black appeared in front of me. Her head was covered, her presence direct and undeniable. She looked straight at me and said:

"Now that you have seen what you were supposed to see, you cannot stay. Wake up!"

And in that instant—I woke up.

It was the first time someone had ever spoken to me so directly in a dream. Have you ever had someone speak to you directly in a dream? As clearly as seeing your own reflection in a mirror—like a head-to-head conversation?

The urgency in her voice and the way she appeared—standing right in front of me, commanding my attention—struck me more than the dream itself. Usually, dreaming feels like witnessing something—like watching yourself on a screen or from a distance. But this was different. The moment she appeared, it no longer felt like I was observing. It feels like I was fully present.

It was around noon when I woke up, and I couldn't stop thinking about it. Shortly after, my mother entered the room to check on me and ask if I wanted to eat something. She could see I was distant—lost in thought. When she asked what was troubling me, I told her the dream exactly as it happened. She listened and gently suggested that maybe I had the dream because I had been sick and tired. She reminded me that if I felt fear, I should pray.

We did not speak about it again—not until 4:53 p.m. that same day.

That afternoon, an earthquake struck Port-au-Prince. More than 200,000 lives were lost, including my father's. When the ground started shaking, we ran outside. Our neighborhood was not directly affected, so we had no idea what had happened beyond. It wasn't until others returned—covered in dust and blood, sharing stories of the collapsed buildings and devastation—that it hit me.

My mother turned to me and said:

"This was your dream!"

I had already forgotten it in the moment—but now it was real, unfolding before our eyes.

My brother Patrick asked about the dream, and my mother repeated it to him. I was grateful she had heard it earlier that day—before the tragedy—because it helped me release the doubt that I might have imagined or invented it after the fact.

Even now, I sometimes ask myself: Was I supposed to do something with what I saw that day? Was there something I could have done to help my father? Could I have changed anything?

I know, deep in my spirit, that everything happens according to a higher plan, for my highest good, and the highest good of all. But the question still visits me from time to time.

Because of that experience—and many others I won't mention here—I have come to understand something essential: Dreams are far more complex than we think. For me, sometimes they are invitations. Messages. Lessons. And sometimes, warnings. I still cannot define dreams fully. But I know now that some of them are not random.

✦ ✦ ✦

Dreams: Conversations Between Realms

These days, I no longer try to guide my dreams the way I did when I was younger. For a long time, I buried this part of me. I used to see faces and names I see in my dreams that do not belong to my waking life. People I have never met here, but whom I recognize across multiple dreams. Sometimes years apart.

I used to journal a lot about my encounters. I did not want to forget, or I believed there was something more. I used to wonder who are these people that return to my dreams—faces I have never known but somehow recognized. I sometimes wonder if we meet others in the dreamworld long before we meet them here. Or perhaps only there...

For me, writing things down anchors memory. But some dreams are unforgettable. And the more conscious I am in a dream, the more present I feel—and the less likely I am to forget.

Therefore, I no longer dismiss what comes in the quiet hours. I listen. And because of the conversations between sleep and soul, I have come to understand that dreams are not simply "illusions."

Have you ever awakened with a dream that stayed with you—not because it made sense, but because it would not let go? Maybe it was just a flash, a feeling, a color, a place. Perhaps it made no sense at all.

Are you curious about your thoughts, or your dreams? Do you ever find yourself fascinated by their symbols, their strange logic, or the way they leave a feeling behind?

The story of Joseph in the Bible, for example, explains how Pharaoh's dream was rich with symbolism. You do not have to believe me here—

but let us explore this possibility: What if dreams can sometimes reveal something important in your life? How would you define them then? Would you dismiss the idea that you might possess a connection to the unseen? A connection that you may not have fully explored yet?

Have you ever wondered why, in many spiritual traditions, connection, clarity, and even initiation often come through dreams? Have you ever been curious enough to ask why?

This simple act of falling asleep—only to suddenly see ourselves somewhere else, or to witness symbols and stories unfold—can that really be just a function of the brain? And if it is, then how does it explain my experience?

Across spiritual traditions—from Egypt to the Himalayas, from the Yoruba to the mystics—dreams were never dismissed. They were doorways, revelations, and soul instructions. Before we had books, we had dreams. Before we had doctrines, we had visions. Maybe this is why this part of us still speaks, even if we do not listen.

I often have conversations with different people, and I have noticed that the busier we become, the less we dream. Some of us are so overwhelmed with stress in waking life that we cannot even sleep deeply enough to recharge.

It is something we are slowly losing.

To return to ourselves, some of us travel across countries, trying to reconnect with the essence of nature—just to find rest.

It is as if the noise of life has become so loud that we can no longer sleep. And when we do dream, all we see is the noise we carry—all the patterns, the symbolism and colors of our doubts. And yet, we do not understand what we see as the connection has been broken.

Dreams: Conversations Between Realms

We suddenly have time for everything else, but not for ourselves. We no longer make time, not even for the sacred rest that dreams require.

Sometimes, we try—we try so hard—to remove something that is simply natural to us. We push it away out of fear, or because of the influence of other belief systems or cultures. Maybe we are afraid of being called "primitive." We have become overly "civilized," cutting ourselves off from everything that once reminded us of our natural knowing. But what we do not realize is that what we are silently giving away is our essence—our natural way of sensing, feeling, intuiting, and understanding.

The path of trusting the unseen runs parallel to this understanding of self. If you are a multidimensional being, you must also understand that you speak in multidimensional ways.

Sometimes, dreams do not arrive in words, but in sensations, silence, shapes, or impossible logic. And if you have no inner root—no place within you that knows how to trust yourself—those messages will pass by unnoticed. Forgotten. Lost.

If you can speak in other ways than words, do not expect all of your answers to come in logical form. Some truths will arrive in waves, in colors, in inner knowing. Learn to listen to the parts of you that speak without words. That is still your voice. That is still your guidance.

We are conscious beings, and that means more than simply being awake—it means we are capable of awareness, perception, thought, and inner reflection.

Scientifically, consciousness refers to our ability to experience the world, to observe ourselves in it, and to assign meaning to what we perceive. It is this very awareness—this spark of knowing—

that makes it possible for us to receive guidance even in dreams.

Because, from my understanding, consciousness does not turn off when the body sleeps; it simply shifts into another state. And in that state, we are still listening. Still learning. Still connected.

Therefore, when symbols appear, when a voice speaks, when something within us stirs—it is not just imagination. It is the intelligence of the soul communicating through the language of dreams.

I cannot tell you what your dreams are here to reveal. But I believe you already know, somewhere within. Tonight, before you go to sleep, ask yourself this: *"If my soul wanted to send me one message tonight, what would it be?"* You might not remember anything tomorrow, but by asking that question, you have opened the door that connects you to the part of yourself you cannot see, but that is always listening...

This chapter is lovingly dedicated to the souls who departed on January 12, 2010—and most especially to my father, Georges W. Leroy, who presence continues to guide my heart beyond time.

CHAPTER 12

THE LINE BETWEEN LIFE AND DEATH

What is life, and what is death?
Have you ever asked yourself these questions—or are you simply living, forgetting to question the gate of your arrival and your departure on this planet?
What does your ticket say? What is the number of your flight, the letter of your seat?
Have you not realized that you are a passenger?
If that is true, then perhaps departure should not be so scary. Perhaps we will not be disappearing but simply landing somewhere else.
For me, life and death are part of the same process. They are unseen forces that create and transform. They are not true opposites. I would even say they are twins. One inhale. One exhale. Both standing at the same door—one opens it, one closes it.
Life is the experience of remembering who we are within the boundaries of time. Death is the moment those boundaries dissolve.
The line between life and death is when you find yourself standing at the same door, making conversation with both twins.
Sometimes, the line between life and death is not always visible. It is not always about a severe

disease or being in a coma. Sometimes, it is emotional, spiritual, or even symbolic. It can show up in a moment of deep pain, a loss of direction, or a silence that feels like something in you has died, even if your body keeps moving.

It is a transformation.

Parts of us have died and been reborn many times. Perhaps we have not paid close attention to those moments.

We often think of death as one final event. But parts of us die all the time. It can be a version of you that once existed—maybe the one who trusted too easily, or the one who lived in fear—has already been buried. And in that same space, something else was born. The strength you carry today, the boundaries you now have, the voice you finally trust—they rose from what had to fall away.

We do not always notice these shifts. Sometimes, we only feel the silence after the storm, and we wonder why we are no longer the same. But this too is a form of death, and rebirth.

Some parts of us have been erased so deeply that we can no longer find them, even in our own memories.

Maybe that is how transformation really happens. Not with fanfare, but with forgetting. The forgetting of who we used to be. The disappearance of the pain that shaped us. The vanishing of versions we no longer needed. If we remembered every detail of every version we have been, maybe we would never have the courage to become who we are now.

So many times, we have been transformed and have touched the line between life and death. Some people walk right up to that line and come back. Others live their whole life numb, never realizing how close they are to losing what truly matters.

The Line Between Life and Death

Understanding that line helps us make peace with both life and death. It reminds us to live more fully, to pay attention, and to trust that there is more than what we can see.

The line between life and death can also be crossed in heartbreak, in illness, in moments where the soul feels like it has no more to give. And yet, somehow—we are still here. Still breathing. Still showing up.

These are the places where transformation begins. And the more we survive these symbolic deaths, the more we understand what it means to truly live.

Trusting the unseen means trusting all the variations and transformations of our lives. But more importantly, it means being aware of them.

✦ ✦ ✦

In many spiritual traditions, guidance through life is not just about making the right decisions. Sometimes, it is about aligning with something deeper.

In Hinduism, it is called *dharma*, which is considered as the path the soul came to walk. In Buddhism, guidance comes through awareness, through seeing clearly and acting mindfully.

In Christianity and Islam, life is guided by divine relationship, prayer, and surrender to a higher will. In Kabbalah, guidance flows from divine light and is meant to heal both the self and the world. Indigenous and African traditions often remind us that guidance is all around us, in dreams, in nature, in the voice of our ancestors, and in the rhythm of the Earth.

Across all of these paths, the message is the same: we are not living passively. Life is not seen as random or meaningless. It is intentional.

And you—what is life for you?

Some experiences have taught me that life, death, and memory are deeply connected. Life is where memories are made. Death is where they are held. And memory itself becomes the bridge between the two. As long as we are alive, we carry the stories, faces, and lessons of those who came before us. When someone dies, they do not vanish, their memory continues to shape how we live, how we love, and what we believe. And even after we are gone, something of us remains through the memories we leave behind.

Yet, a couple of years earlier, I would face another moment—not in a dream, but in the edge-space between life and death—where memory and spirit would teach me something important...

✦ ✦ ✦

On March 18, 2020, I became very ill. Living alone in the U.S., I was often battling sickle cell disease—something that, at the time, felt like a curse.

I was feeling more and more exhausted and started seeing black dots floating in front of my eyes. This is not a poetic description. There were actual black dots—my condition was affecting my vision and eventually led to the loss of the lens in my right eye.

At that point, I had no idea how to manage it all. My job offered no paid time off and no health insurance. So, I had no choice but to keep working, even when I was in pain.

Unfortunately, by pushing myself too hard, my body began to collapse. One night, I remember standing next to my bed when everything started spinning. I lost my balance and fell.

On the floor, my heart began racing—so fast it made me nauseous. I tried closing my eyes to calm myself, but it only made things worse. I could not get up. The room was spinning. It felt like I was trapped in an imaginary rollercoaster that I did not know how to stop.

Then suddenly, I could not breathe properly. My breaths became shorter and shorter.

A coworker happened to call me that night. I reached for the phone and asked to be taken to the hospital.

I was shaking. I was sweating, even with the AC on. My entire body, every muscle, every joint, started hurting. It felt like someone was throwing rocks at me with no mercy.

I arrived at the hospital barely able to breathe. To this day, I only remember getting there. I do not remember being admitted or anything from the first few days. I spent ten days in the hospital, including two days in a coma.

I was conscious again when I woke up in the Intensive Care Unit (ICU), confused, surrounded by machines. There were lines running into my neck, my thigh, my arms—even my feet. There were ventilators, feeding tubes and IV pumps. I was connected to machines in ways I could not understand, suspended between silence and survival.

I remember the moment I opened my eyes for the first time after waking up. My mind was still foggy, and I found myself quietly asking: Where am I?

As my vision began to adjust, I saw a presence standing at the foot of my bed. It had a human form, and for a moment, I thought it was my father—or maybe my mind was trying to assign a familiar face to what I was seeing. Because truly, the face was not visible. It was luminous, almost too bright to see clearly. But the brightness was contained within it. It did not illuminate the room or even cast light on my bed, though it stood so close.

We did not speak with words. Instead, we communicated telepathically, in a way that bypassed sound and entered directly into knowing.

It let me know that I was safe. That was all. But it was enough. The presence stayed for a few seconds, and when I blinked, it faded away.

Have you ever felt a presence you could not explain? Even if it was not as vivid as what I experienced, but have you ever felt, even for a moment that you were not alone?

It was the first time I had ever experienced something like that. But in that moment, I was not even fully thinking about it, my mind was still trying to understand where I was. I was reading the names of doctors and nurses on the whiteboard of the hospital wall.

Later, when I shared the experience with friends and family, they said it must have been because I almost died. Maybe. But I know this was not a dream. My eyes were wide open.

It happened in those very first moments of waking—and I remember it clearly. It could not have been my imagination; my mind was actively trying to understand where I was. I believe it was a visitation. Maybe, it was a presence meeting me in that in-between space where spirit and body reunite. And even now, I carry the peace of that moment with me.

At the time, I did not understand what had happened. But in the years since, I have come to recognize that I had touched a liminal space

The Line Between Life and Death

between memory and eternity.

Waking up in the ICU room after days of unconsciousness felt like I had only blinked—as if time had folded into itself and passed like a dream. But my friends told me otherwise. They told me we had spoken. That they had brought gifts. That they had received text messages from me. I had no memory of any of it.

I would even argue that the text messages were not from me. I could not remember sending them. I could not know that I was *not* there.

Even after I was moved out of the ICU and transferred back to the regular floor, I was happy to see my belongings that the nurses had returned to me. I remember feeling surprised—I could not even recall what clothes I had been wearing when I arrived at the hospital. I called my friends to thank them for the gifts I found by my bed, only to hear: "You already thanked me; I gave you that myself, before they moved you to the ICU."

My friend Monica, to whom I am greatly grateful, who spent the early days with me at the hospital, before the Covid rules' restrictions, later described the conversation we had before she stepped out to grab a cup of coffee and speak with the nurses—and how, shortly after, they urgently called "code blue" to transfer me to the ICU.

I still have no recollection.

Some things my friends shared stories, felt vaguely familiar—like I had seen them in a dream. But other memories were simply… erased. As if a whole section of my life had been removed, silently, without explanation.

The most striking part? I forgot my early university years. To this day, I cannot remember studying Public Relations before I went to law school. I know I studied Public Relations and

Marketing when I was 18 and 19 years old. But, I have no memory of any class, no teacher's name, no friendships, no images.

And yet, there is proof—official records showing I was there, passing my classes.

So, what part of me was communicating, texting and smiling during those days? It seems that part of me was not fully conscious and maybe even fading away.

It makes me wonder: if the body itself does not guarantee consciousness, but it is the unseen part of us that does—then who are we, truly?

Someone is conscious when the brain is actively processing experience and self-awareness in real time. But what does self-awareness really mean? It is the state of being conscious and not just being "awake." Therefore, can it truly be limited to the brain?

Consciousness is not just about having a beating heart and open eyes. It is the ability to be aware of awareness itself. It goes beyond physical presence. It reaches into a deeper knowing of the self, beyond the body.

I understand that science can look at the brain and see activity. It can measure waves, track signals, and monitor reactions. But it cannot show us the "I" who is watching all of it unfold. That part—the one who knows, feels, remembers, and wonders—remains unseen. That is consciousness. And it cannot be fully captured by a scan.

Therefore, consciousness cannot be limited to the brain. We are conscious—but we are not just our brain. We are the ones aware of it.

In this way, the brain is the receiver, and consciousness is the signal. So if consciousness is required for someone to *truly be*—then who are we, really?

The Line Between Life and Death

What began as a medical emergency became, for me, a spiritual invitation. Not because I saw death—but because I saw what the mind cannot hold, and what the spirit will never forget.

This taught me something deep: Not remembering does not mean it did not happen. Just like a dream, a life lived and forgotten is still a life that shaped us.

This experience changed the way I see memory, and by extension—the state of consciousness and spirituality. Because when I was that close to death, everything became distant. My attachments faded. Time dissolved. My body was silent. And my mind released what it could not carry anymore.

It was peaceful—not frightening.

I do not remember feeling any pain, any fatigue—or any sensation at all. It felt as if the mental part of me had stepped away. My state of consciousness was no longer present, and something within me remained only to witness the body. Strangely, it was the waking world that began to feel like a dream.

Since then, I have come to see that death is not the end—it's a doorway. And memory? It is sacred, but also selective. In both dreams and dying, certain things lose importance, and some things stay with us even when the mind forgets.

Now, I understand that remembering is not only mental—it is also spiritual.

For me, awareness returns when the spirit returns. Without it, this physical reality begins to feel like a series of fleeting dreams. We are witnessing, without even being present.

" Once upon a time, I dreamt I was a butterfly, fluttering hither and thither, to all intents and purposes of a butterfly.

PISTIS: The Art of Trusting the Unseen

[...] Soon I awaked, and there I was, veritably myself again. Now I do not know whether I was a man dreaming I was a butterfly, or whether I am now a butterfly, dreaming I am a man."
—*Zhuangzi (Chuang Tzu)*

CHAPTER 13

WHEN WORDS BECOME HOME

I come to believe that: *"To remember love is to remember who you are, for trusting the unseen is also how you learn to love yourself."* But what if the first place you ever felt safe... was a *word*?"

Growing up, I never felt insecure. I was a child surrounded by warmth—by family, by friends, by the kind of love that asks for nothing in return. I was seen. I was appreciated. I was understood; and I carried that with me like a secret light.

Even now, when the world feels heavy or I question my place in it, I close my eyes and return to those memories—not to escape, but to remember what unconditional love feels like. Because they just loved me. Without effort. Without expectation. Without needing me to be anything more than I already was.

I want to take a moment here to honor some of those souls who still live in my heart, no matter the time or distance. Some of my childhood friends and family members, who hold an important place in my memory. They laughed and cried with me at uncalculated moments, when the only language between us was presence and trust.

They held space for me when life was still made of dreams and simplicity. They showed me, more than once, what unconditional love really feels like. And though years, circumstances, and life itself may shift and change, the feeling I carry for them never will. Because they did not just love me—they changed my heart. And for the memories we shared, I am always grateful.

As I grew older, adulthood introduced me to another kind of love. One that came with conditions. One that sometimes asked me to shrink, to prove, to perform. In some relationships, I felt erased—like I had become invisible inside a mirror that once reflected joy. And I did not know how to hold both truths at once: the love I had known and the ache I was carried.

For a time, I forgot the sound of my own inner voice.

During this season, silence felt heavy. Not peaceful, but empty. I had poured so much of my worth into the mouths of others. Waiting for a "You are beautiful." A "You are doing well." A "You are enough." I waited, thinking that maybe if someone else believed it, I could too. But the more I waited, the more I drifted from myself.

I remember when I was nineteen, I was young and unprepared. I was open to love, but unaware of the emotional patterns I was walking into.

I fell in love and stayed in a relationship for four years. It was a constant cycle of cheating, lying, and betrayal. And yet, I stayed.

At some point, I began to believe that this was love: the chaos, the back-and-forth, the blind readiness to forgive. I would silence the voice within me that tried to guide me out. That whisper of wisdom—soft, but persistent—I ignored it. Because I was too busy fighting to be seen, to be loved, to be chosen.

When I received the minimum, I called it

enough. When I was hurt, I told myself it was normal. I no longer believed in love that was pure, safe, or simple. I only knew love as struggle.

Until the day he confessed that another woman was pregnant with his child. Something shifted in me. It was not rage, or heartbreak, or even numbness. It was understanding.

For the first time, I could hear clearly what my inner voice had been whispering all along. And this time—I listened.

I did not scream. I did not curse. I did not collapse. I wished him well, sincerely. Not because I did not feel pain—but because something deeper had awakened in me: a knowing that the lesson had been there all along. That relationship became my punishment, because unconsciously I decided to allow it to be. The longer I tried to save someone else's path, the more I delayed my own happiness.

In many unbalanced relationships, one partner often admits they *"always sensed something,"* or that their *intuition* had been warning them all along.

But what exactly is that voice trying to protect you from? What is it that keeps pulling you away from a path that is draining your energy? Is it a part of you revolting from within? And yet, so often, the noise of the outside world causes us to shut down our inner knowing.

If this voice is with you, even in your darkest moments, trying to pull you away from the tears you are experiencing, and whispering that you will be fine; then, if it is there, like a loyal friend asking for nothing in return, acting only for your good— whether you accept it or not—have you ever wonder what it might reveal if you simply gave it more time to speak? What words might you finally hear—words that teach you something about yourself you never knew, and could never have known before?

After this love chapter had closed, I spent five years being single. Not in isolation, but in exploration. Not rejecting love but rediscovering my own.

I became curious about the peace I felt *after* betrayal. That inner calm led me back to myself. And the more I embraced that peace, the more I realized that when you truly let go, even the echo that once haunted your mind begins to fade. You will try to remember something they said that once wounded you deeply... or something that once brought you joy, and you will find nothing.

It will be silence. A void. A peace.

The same words that once held so much meaning will become weightless. Yet, words are so important in our lives. Why do they hold the power to shape so much of who we are?

Before the world taught us to compete, prove, or perform, many of us were just children—absorbing words without questioning their power. Whether through family members or written across a classroom board, words shaped us. They carried permission, expectation, sometimes judgment, but also hope. And for some of us, they became the first home we ever knew.

And often, you will realize that it is the *words* they spoke—more than their actions—that made you stay in a place you were meant to leave.

It is the words spoken by culture, religion, or tradition that made you hesitate to make a decision that might have saved your life. Sometimes, it is just one word that brings hope—hope that change will come.

But spirituality has taught me that it is no longer the words they said, or the ones that have been said to you that truly matter. What matters now are the

When Words Become Home

words you speak to yourself, and the ones you choose to allow into your life.

Nowadays, there seems to be a new trend—a growing wave of the use of *words* for "positive thinking" and even a daily habit called "affirmations."

It is recommended by almost every guru on the internet. If I did not know better, I might have thought it was just another passing trend or even a hoax. So, I began to wonder if it was part of a new era of thought. After all, every generation brings its own way of thinking.

In French literature and Western philosophy, for example, we had: La Renaissance (*The Renaissance*, approx. 14th–17th century) – a rebirth of art, humanism, and classical ideals. Les Années Lumières (*The Enlightenment*, approx. 1715–1789) – a time of reason, science, and intellectual revolution. Le Romantisme (*Romanticism*, approx. 1800–1850) – an era focused on emotion, nature, beauty, and individual expression.

That is why I love reading and often find myself drawn to art as well—because when you pay close attention, it reflects the ideologies, boundaries, and inner frameworks of the people living during that time.

Therefore, I wonder: are we now living in a mental era where people long to love themselves more? What triggered this sense of lack that makes us crave connection so deeply? Are we simply influencing each other, echoing the same ideas, or is it truly working?

I remember, years ago, finding myself lost again, navigating the aftermath of love and the weight of inner emotions.

I had entered a phase of emotional numbness. I was surviving fears rooted in my identity as a woman: the fear of not being enough, the fear of failing, and the panic that maybe I did not understand life at all...

Then, one morning, still wrapped in sleep, I felt something stir—like a wind passing between two worlds. A thought came, not loud, but steady: *"What if you spoke to yourself the way you wished others did?"* And before I could speak it aloud, I picked up a journal and began writing. I wrote the words I had waited years to hear from someone else—and, somehow, they were enough.

"I am worthy of being loved."

"My presence is enough."

"I trust what I cannot see."

"I forgive myself for all the times I did not know I was learning."

That is when *affirmations* found me. Or maybe... That is when I finally began to listen.

I started to speak to myself again—not with judgment or demand, but with devotion. I whispered truths I once believed instinctively, as a child. Affirmations became a way home.

I then remember that this style of thinking was first introduced to me by my teachers in kindergarten and then continued through elementary and high school.

At the time, the teachers called them *"positive thoughts."* Every week, our teachers would write a positive thought at the top of the classroom board.

In elementary school, and even in parts of high school, we were required to include a positive thought on every homework submission.

These messages were often about work, success, love, self-worth, and God. I attended the same

Methodist Christian school for both elementary and high school, and some of the positive thoughts I still remember are:
- L'effort fait des forts *(French)* – Meaning "Effort makes us strong" or "effort creates success." Depending on how the sentence is used.
- Dieu aime les enfants sages *(French)* – Meaning "God loves kind children."
- Un esprit sain dans un corps sain *(French)* – Meaning: *"A healthy mind in a healthy body."* (Sometimes interpreted philosophically as *"a sound spirit in a sound body"* depending on usage and context. Originally derived from the Latin *"Mens sana in corpore sano."*)

At the time, I did not realize that this last phrase had ancient roots. It reflects the words of Juvenal, a Roman poet from the 1st century AD, carrying a spiritual understanding of the harmony between soul and body, encouraging a healthy and balanced life.

For a long time in my youth, I thought those positive thoughts were simply elegant calligraphy meant to decorate the classroom board. But today, I am grateful I learned them.

They were not affirmations in the way I understand them now: words intentionally directed toward oneself, spoken with awareness and purpose. However, this early practice planted a seed. I was being taught the power of words before I truly understood their meaning. Looking back, I realize that this consistent exposure to uplifting language shaped my inner world. It helped me develop a deeper appreciation for the value of speech and thought, even if I did not yet know I was building the foundation for a conscious affirmation practice.

PISTIS: The Art of Trusting the Unseen

Now, being spiritual is, for me, the discovery of the Self—and, more specifically, the discovery of self-love. To be guided is to become aware of what truly nourishes the soul.

Some of my earlier choices were made out of fear and a lack of self-knowledge. They led to poor emotional connections and extended seasons of unnecessary entanglement. But true inner knowing reveals the truth about ourselves and about our connections.

Trusting the unseen is not about rituals alone. It is about self-awareness. Because to know the Divine is to know ourselves. With that said: is the practice of repeating affirmations truly a new trend, or is it the result of new beliefs shaped by this generation?

Across spiritual traditions, there is a revelation and universal truth: *words are divine instruments of creation.*

In Kemet, Tehuti spoke creation into being. In the Torah: *"Let there be light."* In the Qur'an: *"Be, and it is."* In Hinduism, *Om* is the seed of all sound. In Buddhism, words carry karma. In Taoism, truth goes beyond words... Words are not merely tools of expression but acts of alignment. It is probably why we are so naturally drawn to *words.* We feel reassured when someone speaks to us with kindness. We feel at ease when a politician speaks eloquently, offering hope through promises made in words.

We feel comforted when our parents encourage us. We feel loved when someone we love speaks words of affection. Words align us with our deepest sense of security. But they can also awaken our deepest fears.

We do not always remember moments, but we

When Words Become Home

often remember words, and sometimes, they become our truth without our consent.

Culture, belief systems, and the very programming of our minds are shaped through words. Whether spoken, written, or silently repeated in the mind, words create vibrations that can either heal or harm, build or destroy. We are constantly being influenced by language—from the lullabies we hear as infants to the headlines we read today.

If you have never paused to reflect on the importance of words in your life—today is a beautiful day to do so. Because words are not just sounds. They are not neutral. They are unseen forces, shaping the visible.

From experience, I believe that no matter how intelligent you are, if you find yourself in a country where you cannot speak the language, suddenly, a part of your consciousness feels missing.

It is as if something within you becomes invisible. Your thoughts remain intact. Your ideas still live inside you. But without the ability to express them, you begin to feel like you are disappearing from the space you are in. You are there... but not fully seen. Not fully felt. Not because you lack value, but because language is the bridge between your inner world and the outer one.

And it is at that moment that you understand— words are not just sounds. They are your wings. They give shape to your presence. They allow your soul to breathe into form.

When you lose your ability to speak, you do not become less intelligent—you become less *reachable*. And the more unreachable you feel, the more distant you become from the reality around you.

That is why affirmations matter to me. That is

why self-talk matters. Because the words you use, whether spoken aloud or silently repeated, are how you bring yourself into the room.

So when you speak *your* truth over yourself, you are not being naïve. You are being loyal to the memory of who you were, and to the becoming of who you truly are.

Affirming yourself is an act of wholeness.

It is how your spirit, your soul, and your body say yes to each other. It is the moment you stop waiting for the world to see you because you have already seen yourself.

Affirming yourself is not about pretending or masking fear. Even when born out of uncertainty, the act of speaking life over your being is a holy rebellion against despair. It is a return to your divine authority, to your ability to create, to speak, to become.

When we affirm positivity upon ourselves, we are sculpting the Self. Aligning the image we see, the soul that lives within us and the spirit that longs to be heard. We are tuning the soul, body, and mind into one unified frequency.

Even if the Divine Source remains vast, unknowable, and mysterious, we know this: The Divine speaks. And so do we.

I understand that affirmations are not magic spells; they are mirrors. They reflect what is possible when we stop repeating the noise of fear and start echoing the truth of our origin.

So, speak. Not to convince the world, but to remind your soul that you are already what you seek.

CHAPTER 14

MANIFESTATION: POWER GUIDED BY THE SOUL

Most people are taught that manifestation is about vision boards and willpower... But what if it is not about getting what we want, but *knowing* who we are?

I still remember my very first manifestation. I was probably around three or four years old. I was playing with my three older brothers when, for some reason, I fell and started crying. In response, they decided they would not play with me anymore. They told me I should go play with my dolls instead—that I should play with other girls.

But the problem was... there were no girls for me to play with. So I went into my room, still crying, and I prayed for a little sister. And because I knew it would happen, I told my mother: "I'm going to have a little sister. I asked God, and He said yes."

She was not pregnant at this time, and she laughed a little, thinking it was just a child's imagination. After all, she already had three boys, and then finally me—a girl—so my parents felt complete.

But that memory stayed vivid in my heart. It

became a story we still talk about in my family. My mother always says, "You asked for your little sister." Even my sister knows the story—because while my brothers and I were each born just one or two years apart, she arrived five years after me, while my mother was on birth control. In other words, one or two years after my divine request.

Now, why did I insist on telling my mother that I was going to have a little sister? I cannot fully remember—but one thing is certain: as a child, I *knew* it would happen.

Manifestation is the act of bringing into physical form what has already been created in the spiritual realm. It is not magic—it is spiritual. It is a divine process.

> *"All things are formed in the mind before they appear in the world."*
> —Attributed to Ptah, Memphite Theology.

The act of manifesting is an alignment through the eyes of the Spirit because it is not just about making things appear. It is about coming into alignment with what is already true at the soul level.

To manifest is to take a soul vision—something felt, seen, or known in the unseen world and translate it into matter.

The little sister I asked for already existed in the spiritual world. I just wanted to see her in the physical plan. Now, with what I have come to understand, I believe we already knew each other—and I was simply remembering her.

Maybe, even as a child, I had this knowledge and asked for her. My little sister has been—and still is—the greatest best friend I could have dreamed of.

Manifestation: Power Guided by the Soul

But let's remove all the equations, symbols, and complex formulas that make manifestation seem complicated.

Picture this:

You walk into a totally empty room, apartment, or house. The moment your foot touches the floor, your mind begins to visualize—where your belongings will go, what kind of furniture you will add, how you will make it feel like yours.

Over time, those thoughts begin to take form. What you envisioned starts to manifest physically. You can now touch them.

If, when you walked in, you only imagined a mattress on the floor—that's probably all you will end up with. That, too, is a manifestation.

If you never imagined anything at all, chances are you won't pay attention to what you could create—or even realize that you can. When you do not actively create with intention, you are not truly living—you are passively existing. And what fills your space may not be yours at all, but someone else's manifestation that you have accepted by default.

Along my spiritual journey, I have come to understand that manifestations must be guided by purpose.

We have been taught to want things loudly—to speak them into existence, to claim them, to visualize them so hard they bend reality. But not all desires come from the spirit. Some come from the parts of us still trying to be seen, to be validated, or to be loved.

This is where the path of manifestation splits.

Ego-driven manifestation starts with hunger—with lack. It says: "If I had this, then I would feel worthy. If they saw me, then I would feel real. If I achieved it, then I would finally be enough." It's rooted in the illusion that something external will complete us. It manifests through pressure, and timelines. The ego is loud. It shouts manifestations not because it believes them, but because it's terrified, they are not true.

Soul-guided manifestation begins in stillness. It doesn't chase—it listens. It doesn't declare war on what is. It aligns with what could be. The soul knows when a desire is sacred—when it's not coming from the need to escape who we are, but to fully embody who we have always been.

Where ego says, "I want this to prove I can,"

The soul whispers, "I'm ready to receive what already belongs to me."

The ego wants what it sees. The soul desires what it senses.

We have been taught that we can have everything—to ask for anything without limits.

Imagine a child going to the supermarket with their parents, asking for everything they see—wanting everything without limits.

Manifestation with purpose is not about getting everything you want or having more. It's about becoming more aligned. And when you are aligned, you become a living invitation for what is meant for you to arrive.

Most spiritual masters—those whose names became immortal and whose words sparked revolutions—knew one thing in common: their path. Because they knew who they were and what they came to do, they did not just manifest *everything*. They manifested with purpose and understanding. They asked with precision. And when they called with the Divine force within, it was always for their highest good—and the highest good of all.

In Jesus' story, for example, it says that he

understood the laws of the unseen. He knew the power of miracles, yet he never used them recklessly. His manifestations were not for ego or display—they were always rooted in purpose, in mission, in divine timing.

> *"Do you think that I cannot call on my Father, and he will at once put at my disposal more than twelve legions of angels?"*
> —Matthew 26:53 (NIV)

Jesus wanted to teach that he could have manifested help from the Divine, but by knowing his mission, he chose not to. He respected the balance of divine purpose and the ability to manifest anything at will.

When he passed this knowledge to his disciples, they, too, began to understand their purpose. And this is where the true power lies: in knowing yourself.

When you understand your mission, a balance forms between what is possible and what is purposeful. You do not ask for what merely looks good. You ask for what aligns. Otherwise, you risk creating a labyrinth of desires and insatiable wanting that pulls you further away from knowing your soul. The more you have, the more you will want. The more you gain, the more you may feel the need to prove that you can have even more. But is that truly the purpose of the soul—just wanting more?

It is not because you can, that you must.

Manifestation is a call. A transmission to the divine. Anyone can do it—but only those with clarity of vision and alignment of purpose can do it with *power* and *peace*.

You are not calling something into being out of

nowhere—you are calling it into form from a place beyond time. From the blueprint of your highest self. From the spiritual dimension where everything already exists.

Here's a metaphor for your journey:

Imagine your homeland sends you on a sacred mission to a foreign land. You are briefed. You have been trained. You are told that you will learn from this new culture, and in turn, you will share wisdom from your own. You are given guides, tools, and access to help at any time—all you have to do is *ask*. But you are reminded: you are on a mission. You are an ambassador. Your presence here is intentional.

Now imagine that once you arrive, you forget the assignment. You have been distracted. You meet others—millionaires, priests, artists... You start wanting their lives. You begin to pray for what they have. And because your home government loves you, it grants your request. After all, the condition was: ask and you shall receive. They do not want you to feel alone or forgotten.

And because you forgot who you are—and your purpose—you start asking for everything, more and more. You feel like you have broken some invisible code. But something still feels off:

You get the money—but feel empty.

You manifest a relationship—but feel unseen.

You take the spiritual path—but still feel lost.

This, is because you did not ask from knowing, but from disconnection.

Your manifestations were delivered... but without alignment, they only deepen the void.

This is why some people struggle to understand how someone with money and power could ever consider taking their own life—or why anyone would believe that wealth and status don't

Manifestation: Power Guided by the Soul

guarantee happiness. But the reason is simple: peace and happiness come from alignment with your true self, not from performance, possessions, or the alternative realities we have been conditioned to chase.

In marketing, for example, they often say that the best product is the one that meets a real need—because it is intentional, purposeful, and aligned. Confucius also said: *"Choose a job you love, and you will never have to work a day."*

Because alignment always brings clarity and peace. Again, manifestation is a call. A transmission to the divine. But when you call, do you know who you are?

Do you know what you are here for?

Imagine calling to request a bottle of water. The response is simply: We will deliver it—but please give us your name and your address for delivery. But you do not know either—yet you keep asking. Without this awareness, your call lacks identity.

Without self-awareness, your manifestation becomes a request without clear direction. Yes, the Divine still hears it—because it is part of you. Your energy speaks, your intention speaks, and if you insist, you might even receive what you asked for.

But that does not mean it is aligned.

Sometimes, we manifest things from a place of fear, emptiness, or comparison. And when those manifestations arrive, we find ourselves confused. Unfulfilled. Disconnected. We start to ask: *Why did I receive this if it does not feel good for me?*

The answer is simple but often overlooked: you were not aligned with your soul when you asked. You were aligned with your fear, your ego, or someone else's expectations.

I am not exempt from this. I have had to unlearn ego-driven calls, and return to my own soul many times. This is why manifestation must come from awareness.

When your soul speaks, it does not ask for excess or illusion. It asks for what will help you grow, expand, and return to yourself. Without that clarity, you risk calling in something that satisfies your temporary craving but leaves your spirit untouched.

So if something feels wrong—even though you once wanted it—pause. Ask for clarity. Try to create a connection with the unseen to truly understand your desire.

When the connection is created, you might receive an answer—but sometimes, that answer comes as a redirection.

Pistis is trust beyond understanding.

If you believe you can receive *everything* you ask for without honoring divine order, spend some time in nature and observe how it works.

If everything in nature received everything at once, there would be chaos, because there is balance. There is timing. There is sacred restraint. And that same order applies to us.

This is why connecting with yourself, with the unseen and the Divine Source is so important.

When you are rooted in that connection, clarity begins to rise. You start to recognize when it is your ego or your fear speaking, rather than your soul.

Understanding comes. Not all at once, but through moments of stillness, reflection, prayers and meditations. And from that place of inner knowing, you begin to ask differently. You begin to receive differently. Not just from desire, but from alignment.

Often, we try to escape our current reality because we think it is punishment. But many of those difficult moments are actually the most vibrant colors in the tapestry of our becoming. They are not mistakes. They are part of the sacred design.

We are more blessed than we think. More loved than we can imagine. And more guided than we can yet perceive.

> *"Three times I pleaded with the Lord to take it away from me. But He said to me, 'My grace is sufficient for you[...]'"*
> —2 Corinthians 12:8-9 (NIV)

The story of Paul in the Bible—a healer, a miracle worker—received an aligned response instead of a healing.

Apostle Paul is speaking about a personal suffering he refers to as "a thorn in the flesh." He does not specify what it is—some believe it was a physical illness, others think it was emotional, spiritual, or even persecution. Whatever it was, it caused him pain.

Paul says that he pleaded with God *three times* to remove it from him. But instead of taking it away, God answered: *"My grace is sufficient for you, for my power is made perfect in weakness."*

This is not a story of unanswered prayer—but of *divine redirection*. Paul learned that healing does not come through removal but through understanding. Paul wanted the pain gone. However, he learned that he could still rise, still lead, still carry his purpose *with* what he believed was a pain.

Would you understand this kind of answer? Or would you be like the child in the supermarket asking for *everything*?

We chase everything because, deep down, we believe that having it all will finally prove that we are enough. Isn't it?

We are in a material world—a world of perceived lack. Thus, whenever we lack something, we tend to focus on it more than the millions of other things we already have.

Think about it—you are a spiritual being, far above the material, and yet, so often, the first thing we try to manifest is money.

But what is money, really?

It's paper. A human invention. Given artificial value in a market system to facilitate trade. It is not truth—it is a tool. And yet, we treat it like salvation.

We pray for more and more of it. We lose sleep.

We neglect ourselves, our families, and our health... chasing this illusion. We believe that if we just have enough of it, people will see us more, love us more, respect us more.

But what if you think about who you are? What if you stop chasing an illusion and start embodying your power?

You would know that you are already abundant. Not because of what you have, but because of what you are. You would no longer manifest from scarcity. You would manifest from sovereignty. From divine purpose.

Money would no longer be your master—it would become your servant. Illusion would bend before *your* truth. Because with the Divine, you are a co-creator.

May wisdom guide you home to that truth.

You do not attract abundance by chasing it. You step into abundance when you know that you are abundant. You are already whole. You already possess the code. You already came equipped.

In today's world, especially in this new era of social media and spiritual trends, it seems like everyone wants to be rich. And to be clear—there is nothing wrong with wealth itself. Often , the issue is *how and why* people are chasing it. The danger is not just wanting wealth—the danger is forgetting who you are while chasing what they have.

Some people are truly called to wealth. It is part of their soul's blueprint. They are meant to steward resources, to create, to build, and to influence. For them, the inspiration flows naturally. They receive the vision, the code, the creativity. Their abundance is aligned because it is rooted in purpose. It is their soul's contract to learn about wealth.

But others begin to copy the external path, without asking if it matches their inner truth. And yes, they might succeed—on the surface. But the journey feels heavy. They struggle with emptiness, burnout, or regret. Why? Because the desire was ego-driven. It was fueled by comparison, not calling.

Some people become wealthy almost without realizing it—because they were simply responding to a divine invitation. They kept creating what they were guided to create. They were not obsessed with being rich—they were aligned with being true. And the abundance followed.

Others try to manifest from a place of lack. They speak affirmations with their mouth, but their soul is disconnected. That kind of manifestation rarely sustains itself. It may produce something temporarily, but it leaves them spiritually unsatisfied.

As a child, I believed in miracles. I used to pray for healing when I was sick. I was told to pray harder. To pray with more intensity. Like something was missing—or like God had not heard me yet.

But here's *my* truth: Divine grace was sufficient for me. And my pain... it served a greater purpose—one I could not have imagined. Without it, this book may not have been written. Without it, I may have walked paths that were not mine.

Just because something is possible does not mean it is purposeful. Forget what you have been told. Forget the rituals. Forget the trends. When manifesting with what is aligned with your purpose, with your true self—the response will bring continued freedom, clarity, and peace.

Sometimes we manifest what we think will bring material comfort, but those are fleeting pleasures. True alignment delivers something far greater: freedom, wisdom, and deep inner peace—with everything else arriving as a complementary gift to that package.

And remember—your purpose has nothing to do with religion, and not even necessarily with being 'spiritual.' Religions are interpretations—filters passed down through time. Some people may have never heard of any of these concepts and still be perfectly and successfully aligned with themselves.

Your purpose is your own alignment. It is the inner truth that makes you feel whole, that makes you feel *you*.

The Divine Source is not reserved for the elite, the righteous, or the chosen. It is universal. Accessible. Equal. It is part of you. And through every age, the Divine has spoken through all people—not just priests, pastors, spiritual teachers or prophets. The question is not who is called. The question is who is listening. So take a breath. Go inward. Ask not just what you want, but who you are when you ask.

PART III

EMBODIMENT THROUGH THE ACT OF LIVING

Focus: bringing the mystical into the practical, living as a vessel of divine guidance.

PISTIS: The Art of Trusting the Unseen

INTRODUCTION
Living the Unseen

This third part of the journey is an invitation to embodiment. The word embodiment comes from the idea of giving "body" or "form" to something. Therefore, this embodiment allows what is unseen (faith, wisdom, love, Spirit) to take form in how we carry ourselves, speak, relate to others, and move through life.

Not long ago, I found myself at a crossroads that felt strangely solitary. I wanted to learn to trust my inner voice, to discern all the voices that are often competing for my attention. Then, I realized that recognition and alignment would remain incomplete if they did not take form in the way I lived and in the choices I am making when doubts arrive. Because very often, I feel the wonder of recognizing the unseen, I taste the freedom of hearing its guidance, but I hesitate to embody it...

In these chapters, you will see what that embodiment means to me. It flows in my practice of being present, in the stillness of silence that becomes my teacher, in the gratitude that transforms the smallest moments into great ones. It rises when I let Spirit lead my steps through both certainty and uncertainty, weaving destiny and choice into a dance that is uniquely mine.

This embodiment, very often, it is not about becoming something new but remembering to live as who we already are. It is found in the conversations we hold, the pauses we take, the courage with which we say yes or no. It is found in the ordinary spaces of life, where the unseen takes form through the way we move through the world.

If Part I called us to awaken to the unseen, and Part II called us to trust its voice, then Part III calls us to live it. To carry it in our heart, in our hands, in our words, and in our very presence. For in the end, the journey of *Pistis* is not only about trusting the unseen but also becoming a living reflection of that trust.

CHAPTER 15

BOUNDARIES AS SPIRITUAL TOOL

I did not begin this journey with answers. I began with discomfort. With a sense that something was off, even when everything appeared fine. I began with the feeling that my peace was too often negotiated. I did not know how to hold it without guilt.

Some lessons are slowly unfolded, through experiences that unsettle us, through people who mirror something back to us, or through moments that make us question what we allow and why. This is how I started understanding boundaries as a spiritual tool. It was not a rule that was taught to me, but the *truth* I had to *feel*.

> *"Above all else, guard your heart, for everything you do flows from it."*
> —Proverb 4:23.

This scripture changed the way I understood boundaries. It does not say guard your heart out of fear but, because your heart is sacred. Because everything you carry, everything you give, and everything you become flows from within; and that inner space must be protected like a sanctuary.

For a long time, I believed that setting

boundaries meant building walls. I thought it was something you did to protect yourself when you were afraid or tired of being hurt. And for many, that is where the journey begins. But I have come to understand that boundaries are not a rejection of others, they are a recognition of Self.

Growing up in a family that taught me strong values, I was guided by principles of respect, discipline, and obedience. And for that, I am grateful. Those instructions shaped me. They helped me navigate life with kindness and reverence for others. But as a child, I was not taught how to say no.

To say no was sometimes seen as disrespectful. I—like many children—was expected to agree with the parents, listen to the teachers, and yield to anyone older than me, regardless of how I felt inside. There was no space to question, no room to resist. And while this instilled humility, it also planted confusion to trust my voice if it disagrees with authority.

I now accept part of that teaching—and I lovingly reject the part that silenced my inner compass. Because what I have come to realize is that a sense of obedience without a sense of self, leads to hesitation, self-doubt, and quiet resentment.

Today, I am witnessing something different in the next generation. My little niece, for example, has a bold and honest spirit. Even at a young age, she will tell you "no" if she does not like something. She knows when she is uncomfortable—and she says so. I find this both courageous and wise. I often encourage her parents to let her keep her voice. To let her learn that boundaries are not rebellion, but a form of self-respect.

When children learn that "no" is not a weapon,

but a tool, they also learn that others have the right to say it too—and that a "no" from someone else is not rejection, but *truth*.

Therefore, children can be raised honoring both themselves and others without carrying guilt or offense in the presence of honesty.

Because of my own child's experience, I would say now that understanding the importance of helping children trust their inner compass and feel comfortable with boundaries is essential. Often, in certain moments of our lives, we may feel the urge to say no—but we do not—because of a lack of inner trust. Sometimes, we find ourselves reflecting on a past situation and thinking, "I should have said no. Why did I stay silent?" Upon deeper reflection, we realize that we did not set a boundary because we were afraid—afraid of rejection, of being seen differently, or of what the future might hold if we did not comply.

Trusting the unseen means discovering a power within you that aligns with your truth and will never let you down. It allows you to say no with confidence, knowing it reflects your truth and what makes you feel safe and at peace. No matter the circumstances, the outcome will ultimately support your well-being. In this space, fear no longer has a place—especially the kind of fear that makes you settle for less or accept what is not meant for your peace.

Boundaries are not barriers. They are structures of sacred energy.

When you walk a spiritual path without honoring your own boundaries, you begin to mistake self-abandonment for humility. You say yes when your soul says no. You stay in places long after the lesson has passed. You begin to confuse endurance with love. But the soul knows, and the

PISTIS: The Art of Trusting the Unseen

spirit speaks—every time.

Sometimes boundaries are not decisions we make. They are whispers from within—urging us to realign. To leave what no longer fits. To decline what is not meant to be ours. When we ignore these whispers, we wander into paths that are not meant for us—or stay too long in classrooms where the lesson has already been learned.

One of the gifts of the unseen is discernment—knowing what is for you and what is not. Boundaries are the expression of that discernment in action. They are the way you say: *"I know who I am, and I honor what I carry. I will no longer hand it over carelessly. This path aligns with my truth. That one does not."* Without boundaries, you live reactively rather than intentionally. To have no boundaries is to abandon yourself in the name of others.

Boundaries are how we draw a sacred circle around what we love, including ourselves. They are how we create space to hear the Divine whisper through us. They are how we stay in rhythm with our truth.

Considering most of the spiritual scriptures, even the Divine sets boundaries. Creation itself began with limits—light from darkness, sky from earth, sea from land. Harmony flows through structure.

So now, I do not apologize for choosing silence over striving. Stillness over pleasing. Peace over pretending. Your boundaries are not an ending—they are a homecoming.

Across spiritual traditions, boundaries are not seen as rejection but as alignment. In Christianity, Jesus set boundaries: he withdrew from crowds to pray alone (Mark 1:35), refused to perform miracles on demand (Luke 23:8-9), and walked away from those who only sought him for spectacle.

In Buddhism, the *Eightfold Path* teaches right action and right mindfulness, which require setting limits on what we absorb, say, and do to protect our inner peace.

Hinduism teaches *Dharma*, a spiritual duty that includes respecting one's own path and not interfering in the karma of others.

> *"It is better to do one's own dharma, even though imperfectly, than to do another's dharma, even though perfectly. It is better to die in one's own duty; the duty of another brings fear."*
> —Bhagavad Gita 18:47

It explains that respecting your own path is spiritually vital. Interfering in another's *dharma*—even with good intentions—can disturb divine order. This is an ancient affirmation of boundaries as spiritual wisdom and tool to stay aligned with our true selves.

In Kabbalah, divine energies are held in balance by *Gevurah*—restraint—reminding us that love without form can become chaos.

Taoism speaks of flowing with the *Way*, and honoring the natural boundaries of things without forcing outcomes.

Hermetic wisdom teaches that everything is energy, and to stay in divine frequency, we must set energetic boundaries that preserve our alignment.

In Yoruba thought, every person is born with *Aṣe*—a divine life force or power of command and manifestation. Respecting one's *Aṣe* means living in alignment with one's destiny (*Ayànmọ*), which requires honoring personal energy and not allowing others to misuse or drain it.

In Indigenous spiritualities, sacred circles are drawn to define space, intention, and spiritual focus—what enters must be conscious and respectful.

In all of these paths, boundaries are not selfish. They are spiritual intelligence in motion. They are how the soul preserves its rhythm, its knowing, and its balance.

I used to explain my 'no' as if it needed permission. I would cushion it, soften it, wrap it in reasons so I would not be misunderstood. But a true boundary needs no apology. It is not an attack, it is *truth*.

And what does that really mean—your *truth*? It means living in harmony with what brings you peace. It means choosing what is aligned with your body, your values, your energy. It means not betraying yourself to make someone else feel comfortable.

Before I learned how to speak my boundaries, my body was already doing the talking. I just did not know how to listen. I used to be in pain when I was uncomfortable. I used to experience anxiety in my chest after agreeing to something I did not want to do, a tightness in my throat when I swallowed my discomfort. There was an exhaustion I carried home after pretending to be okay—these were all forms of communication. These were signs that I had stepped out of alignment, that I had left my truth somewhere behind just to be accepted.

But *truth* is not selfish, it is balanced.

We speak often about generosity, compassion, charity. But what is charity when it comes from depletion? What is kindness when it leaves you empty?

Boundaries as Spiritual Tools

Even giving must come from a place of inner agreement. If you are offering help, a favor, or even a donation—and there is a pinch inside you, a calculation, a hesitation rooted in guilt or pressure—pause. That is not charity. That is negotiation with your peace. Before agreeing to anything, first take a moment to understand why you feel the way you do. If it does not feel genuine, pause and speak honestly with yourself. You deserve your own truth and clarity.

Sometimes we break our own boundaries and agree to things because we are afraid of being seen as a bad person. Or because we were taught to always be kind and obedient. Or simply because we feel like we have no other choice.

I come to understand that there is nothing divine in sacrifice that leaves you bitter. Therefore, learn first how to balance your own needs. Learn how to offer yourself the peace you are so eager to extend to others. Then, what you give will flow from abundance—not pressure. You will help not because you have to, but because it is in harmony with who you are.

The unseen can only flow into a vessel that is ready to hold it. If your energy is constantly leaking—through overcommitment, people-pleasing, or emotional exhaustion—you will not have space for divine insight, creative inspiration, or inner peace. Boundaries are how you seal your energy, so you can receive fully.

The voice of the unseen is subtle. It does not shout over chaos or override your will. If your life is constantly filled with people's expectations, noise, guilt, or emotional clutter, it becomes harder to hear what is true for you. Boundaries create the stillness necessary for spiritual clarity.

To walk with the unseen is to walk with wisdom.

And wisdom requires you to know where you begin and where you end. Just as the earth has gravity and the ocean has shores, your spirit needs structure. Boundaries are not about limitation but honoring divine order. In spiritual terms, they are a form of reverence for your own being. You do not allow what is misaligned to enter your space—not out of fear, but out of love.

I now understand and fully accept that boundaries are not a way of keeping others out, but a way of keeping myself aligned. They protect the light I carry, the lessons I have integrated, and the truth I have remembered.

They are how I say yes to my path without apology, and no without guilt. Every time I honor what feels true within, I affirm that my soul is worthy of peace. And when I honor the boundaries of others, I recognize the sacredness of their path, too.

Because in the end, boundaries are not the end of connection, they are the beginning of it, redefined through clarity, respect, and spiritual alignment. And once the space has been made sacred, we are invited to inhabit it. Fully. Fiercely. Moment by moment.

CHAPTER 16

THE PRACTICE OF BEING PRESENT

The classroom clock ticked.
The silence was heavy, and we were so focused on our work that it was the only sound we could hear. My eyes were fixed on my book. The teacher was reading silently and had asked us to do the same. In a few minutes, she would randomly choose someone to explain the text and perform both a grammatical and logical analysis of what we had read.

I always liked this part of school. It was calm. I was comfortable.

Suddenly, my nose and eyes began to burn. My body started to itch. I was coughing... My classmates were coughing too...

We heard noises coming from nearby classrooms—shouting, movement. The teacher quickly ordered us to get down to the ground and carefully cover our mouths and noses. Other students and teachers were running past our door in panic. Then we heard the principal's voice through a megaphone, instructing us to leave the classroom immediately and find air—warning us to keep our heads low to avoid the gas that had been released around the school.

I was nine or ten years old. That was the first

time I experienced the effects of tear gas. I did not know what it was. We stayed on the floor for a moment, then made our way to the outdoor basketball court, where we were given lemon and water to ease the burning sensation. Some teachers were helping children who were struggling with breathing or asthma. Soon after, parents began arriving to take their children home. It was one of the most shocking moments of my childhood.

I grew up in a country where political instability was part of a collective memory known by generations before and after mine. Fear, therefore, was part of our daily existence. We never knew what might happen in the streets, at school, or even in our own homes. So, I grew up believing that *being present* meant *being alert*.

Like soldiers who learn to master their fear and react swiftly under pressure, many of us grew up with an unconscious awareness of survival. My version of *presence* was not stillness or peace. It was scanning the room, reading body language, noticing movements, and positioning myself to act without panicking.

Years later, in 2021, I was living in the U.S. with two roommates. One morning, while we were eating, their dog's bandage fell off and blood began to pour. My roommates froze. One of them was in shock and started to cry. I responded instinctively by telling them what I needed to stop the bleeding, improvising a bandage from what we had on hand and it worked. The dog was able to see the veterinarian the next day, and the vet confirmed that what I had done had helped.

They then asked me if I had gone to nursing or medical school, but I had not. I simply *knew* I could not panic. That was my version of presence: the ability to assess, act, and take control of the

The Practice of Being Present

moment.

For many of us, especially those who come from places where safety is not guaranteed, presence has never been just a gift. It was more seen as a *duty*. A survival instinct taught by parents and teachers as early as possible.

Later in life, I read quotes like *"The present is a gift"* from different authors and through countless publications, and perhaps you have too. If so, this chapter is not here to repeat what you have already been told, but to offer a continuation, maybe, a deeper layer.

Because of the awareness I was taught, and through my evolving relationship with my inner compass, I have come to understand that the present is not only a gift, but also a teacher, and a reflection of what we choose to see, to be and to stay.

When we act to escape danger or fear, we are rarely truly present. We can react so quickly that there is little room for conscious awareness, unless we have practiced those situations often enough to know how to respond safely with intention.

This made me realize that my understanding of being present solely as an act of survival or reflex was not entirely true. Every time I acted under pressure or by instinct, I would later understand that it was a mechanism, an automatic response rather than a conscious, reflected one. Now I understand that being present is more than giving, saying, thinking, or doing something automatically.

Every second we are awake, our attention becomes the brushstroke painting the next scene of our life through words, thoughts, actions and reactions. Therefore, being present is not just a reaction, a feeling, or a response to time, but a practice. It is how we meet every moment in our life with awareness. And, the present cannot be reduced to time, for time can sometimes be passive. The present is participatory. It does not wait to arrive, it waits to be noticed. In every moment, in every word, and in every thought, we can practice being present.

If you have ever been in a gathering, a church, a conference, or a meeting, where people stand, sit, or move when instructed, you may notice that your conscious mind shifts into an automatic pilot mode. Like everyone else, you will follow the flow. You will see what you are told to see and will notice only what you are told to notice.

This is *fragmented presence*—when the body is here, but the mind is not free.

I have lived days where my body was in a place, but my mind was somewhere else grasping at what could be or grieving what was lost. I now understand that the soul cannot stretch into tomorrow. It only breathes here.

Spiritually, the present is what connects us to the world within, the world around, and the world beyond. It is the meeting point for all dimensions—above, beneath, inside, and outside. It is the moment of choice. And in that choice, we decide what matters, what holds weight, what stays, and what dissolves. The present moment is the space in which we define how we see ourselves, and what we allow to shape us. Because it is this awareness that allows everything else to unfold.

Let us take a simple example. Consider an employee working under a clock-hour system. That person has a set number of hours each day in which they must be present, focused on their

The Practice of Being Present

responsibilities to be compensated. If their awareness drifts, if their presence is fragmented, then their productivity, and ultimately their purpose in that task begin to weaken. Their presence requires them not only to be there physically, but also to be aware of their function.

The same is true on a spiritual level.

When our awareness shifts away from our inner being, when we go through daily tasks disconnected from our inner self; we lose balance. We perform without depth. We exist, but we are not alive. So, presence is not just a relationship with time and the physical, it is a relationship with consciousness. And the deeper that relationship becomes, the more integrated and whole we feel.

I know this because I have experienced it beyond the waking world. In a lucid dream, for example, I am conscious that I am dreaming. I am aware. I can understand what is happening and, most importantly, I can remember.

That state of presence is therefore not limited to the physical body. It is not tied to whether my feet are on the ground. It is connected to my level of awareness within the experience itself—whether physical, mental, or spiritual. This is why two people can share a moment, but only one remembers it. Or why we can be in a room, but leave with nothing emotionally or spiritually absorbed. It is not just about being there. It is about the awareness we bring into the moment. That is what makes the experience real. That is what makes it stay.

The present is considered a gift because it is what we currently have. But if we are not aware of what we have, it is as if we have nothing at all. What makes the present a gift is the awareness we bring to it, and not merely the moment or the passage of time itself.

> *"Do not dwell in the past, do not dream of the future, concentrate the mind on the present moment."*
> — Buddha

I also understand that the present moment is never empty. It is rich with invisible life. It is the field where heaven touches earth, where thought becomes form, and where truth finds a home.

Understanding when you are present brings clarity. Sometimes, it transforms you into a quieter, more reflective person because you begin to understand the meaning within each moment of your life. You become conscious of your actions, your thoughts, and your decisions, and how each one can either align you with or pull you away from harmony with yourself.

Even the systems of laws, there are rules with age limits, not only because time defines us, but also because awareness does. In our youth, we are often less conscious, less aware and less able to understand the weight of our actions. This is why, in criminal law, intention matters. A person's mental state—what they knew, understood, or meant—is often more important than the act itself. Entire legal doctrines exist to measure the level of conscious awareness behind a decision.

This, too, is a reflection of spiritual truth: being present is not about where your body is, it is about what your consciousness is holding. The soul's presence is measured not by movement, but by meaning.

The practice of being present is the practice of awakening. It is not about perfection, but awareness. When you return to the moment with intention, you return to yourself.

The Practice of Being Present

The Parable of the Clay Cup
There was once a young woman who had traveled far in search of wisdom. Her heart was full of questions. She had studied many books, followed many voices, and filled her days with teachings. Still, something in her felt unsettled, like she had collected truths but had not yet lived them.

She decided to go to a quiet mountain village to seek wisdom. She had heard of an old potter who had lived for many seasons and was said to shape more than just clay but understanding.

When she arrived at his humble home, the potter invited her in and offered her tea. The young woman, eager and restless, began to speak. She spoke of wanting clarity, how she wished to know her purpose. But as she spoke—about her goals, her studies, her struggles, her past, her fears—he quietly poured the tea into a small clay cup... and kept pouring.

The cup overflowed. Tea spilled across the table and soaked her sleeve. She gasped.

"Be careful. You are wasting it!" she said, startled.

The potter smiled gently.

"And so are you," he replied.

She looked at him, confused.

"You carry too much from yesterday and worry too much about tomorrow. Your cup is full. So full, there is no space for this moment."

He poured a fresh cup and placed it in her hands.

"This cup is now. You must be *present* enough to receive it."

In that silence, she understood.

PISTIS: The Art of Trusting the Unseen

❖ ❖ ❖

The present moment is like that cup—simple, open, and sacred. But too often, we approach life already full. Full of regrets, full of planning, full of stories we have not yet let go. And in doing so, we miss the awareness of *now*.

We are living in a time where everything outside of us is designed to pull us away from within. Notifications, timelines, headlines, and endless scrolling—all constantly asking for our attention. We are praised for how fast we respond, how much we produce, how visible we remain—yet so much of it is an automatic response, a reflex to life itself.

In a world like this, stillness begins to feel unfamiliar, even uncomfortable. We check our phones before we check in with ourselves. We react before we reflect. And slowly, without realizing it, we become strangers to our own inner rhythm. Our attention is now divided across platforms, conversations, and curated noise. The result is not just distraction; it is disconnection. Not from others, but from the voice within us that only speaks in silence.

Presence asks us to pause, to pour out what is no longer needed, and to hold space for what is unfolding. Because life is not waiting to begin, it is already happening. The more we practice presence by being aware, the more clearly, we can receive what is meant for us.

Like the clay cup, we do not need to hold everything. We only need to consciously hold this moment.

CHAPTER 17

THE WISDOM OF SILENCE

At a young age, every time I became sick, the pain often made it difficult for me to speak. In those moments, I was not choosing silence, I was forced into it. But over time, silence became a space that held me while the pain passed.

When I was younger, all I wanted was relief. Beyond pain medication, I followed whatever the doctors told me. Because I knew my condition was connected to my blood cells and the flow of oxygen, quiet breathing became a natural practice. I learned to regulate my breath during episodes, to stay calm even when my body was in distress. I did not realize it at the time, but those moments were early forms of meditation, and they would one day become my spiritual foundation.

As the years passed, I noticed that silence was not just a coping mechanism, but a doorway to connection. My connection to my inner self. I later understood that I could not force or manipulate my way into spiritual awareness, as it rises when there is space for it. Silence was the condition that allows the unseen to *become visible* in my life; not necessarily through my eyes, but through my inner knowing.

When I practice connecting with myself and

with the Higher Power—by whatever name you call it—I feel most aligned in silence. I visited many churches: some where people prayed aloud together, declaring their faith in unison, and others where stillness was honored. But my clearest spiritual connection always came in quiet.

Perhaps it is because my earliest encounters with the unseen happened in silence, alone, in my sick child's bed, where I could not speak, but I could listen. I would close my eyes and let my breath lead me to a comfort I could not find anywhere outside of myself.

In those moments, I would talk to converse. Not in the way I would pray to request something, but in a way that felt like a whisper between souls. A transformative exchange between my pain and some *Presence* that understood it.

There were days when I could not walk at all. When I was completely dependent on my family to move me, care for me, and even carry me to the bathroom. I would eat in bed, unable to sit properly because every movement caused pain. So, I spent many days in silence, wrapped in pain.

I missed days, sometimes weeks, of school. I could not play like the other children. I could not run for long, swim, or do anything that might exhaust me because my body could collapse, sending me into a crisis. At any moment, day or night, I could fall sick. If it was too hot or too cold, if I exercised, if I walked barefoot too long in the house, anything could trigger it.

My family was always on alert, watching my actions and diet, trying to protect me from further suffering. But in those moments, silence was my comfort. Whenever I was sick, I could not bear noise. If my siblings were shouting or playing loudly, it felt as if the pain in my body intensified with every sound. I would start to cry, and my mother would have to tell them to keep quiet. They hated that. We were all children, and sometimes they did not understand why they had to stay still just because I was resting.

As we grew older, they would sometimes tease me about how I cried whenever they made noise while I was sick. I would laugh along with them, but deep down, I do not think anyone ever truly understood why silence mattered so much to me. Because over time, I came to see that silence was not a void. It was a presence of its own; and with each return to that inner space, I became more attuned to the unseen rhythm of life moving through me.

I began to realize that I did not feel alone or afraid when I was by myself. In fact, I could spend hours in silence and feel completely recharged, as if I had slept for hours. Sometimes people do not understand why I enjoy being alone and quiet, but for me, it has become a need, just like eating or drinking.

Being silent, alone, and taking deep breaths feels to me like sinking into warm water in a bathtub. It is peaceful. It is refreshing; and in that stillness, I meet myself.

> *"Be empty of worrying. Think of who created thoughts! Why do you stay in prison when the door is wide open? Move outside the tangle of fear-thinking. Live in silence."*
> —Rumi (The Essential Rumi)

When we are silent—internally and externally—we create space for deeper knowing to emerge. Not everything needs to be analyzed or spoken to be understood. In silence, clarity does not arrive through thinking harder, but through becoming still enough to *see*.

Sometimes we overshare or respond too quickly, not because we are ready, but because we are afraid. Afraid of being misunderstood. Afraid of seeming distant. Afraid of what silence might make others assume about us. But silence is not avoidance. It is another way of trusting the unseen. It is the space where we allow what is true to rise without force. When we naturally choose silence, it is a way of saying: *"I trust that I do not need to explain everything right now. I trust that what needs to be known will reveal itself in time."* In that pause, we honor our intuition, our timing, and the unfolding of things beyond our control.

Wisdom is not always what you say. Sometimes, it is what you *choose not* to say.

I have already shared how powerful words can be—how affirmations shape the self and carry creative force. But I have also come to understand that not all power is spoken. Some of them are held. Some of them are vibrational, beyond intelligible language. Silence, to me, holds an energy that words cannot always carry.

Silence is where I meet the inward world. It is where the breath slows, the heart listens, and the soul remembers without having to translate itself. In silence, there is no performance. There is no pressure to be understood. There is only the frequency of presence—subtle, invisible, yet deeply alive.

"In silence, we hear what the world forgets to say."
—Traditional Native Teaching

The Wisdom of Silence

When I enter silence with intention, I do not feel alone. I feel held. Because silence does not abandon. It embraces. It is the sound of the Spirit that speaks without needing language. And in those moments, I do not need to affirm anything out loud. The silence affirms me.

> *"Be still and know that I am God."*
> —Psalm 46:10 (NIV)

In its essence, silence is not just the absence of sound. It is a space where no demands are made, no explanations are needed, and no expectations weigh the soul. And yet, in the world we live in today, silence has become rare.

Everything is loud, our schedules, our responsibilities, our thoughts. We wake up, prepare, go to work, return home, tend to the next task, and repeat the cycle again and again.

Life moves fast, often without pause, and in that rhythm, we slowly disconnect from the parts of us that can only be heard in stillness. But then something unexpected happens—a loss, an illness, a heartbreak, or even a single overwhelming day—and suddenly, we seek silence. Not because we want to escape the world, but because we instinctively long to reconnect with something within.

In moments of frustration or fatigue, you may see someone take a deep breath, step away from a room, or simply hold their heads and close their eyes. These are not random habits, they are soul reflexes. They reveal a longing to communicate with the unseen self, the part of us that holds clarity, peace, and presence beyond words.

We may think we are removing ourselves from the physical situation, but what we are truly doing is returning inward, searching for an embrace, for a knowing beyond logic, for the soundless language of the spirit that knows how to hold us when the outer world cannot. Here, in this inner sanctuary, time slows, breathing deepens, and the noise of the mind softens just enough for us to feel safe.

Can you recall a time when something happened and you suddenly felt the need to be in silence, alone with yourself, in order to feel better? As if, inexplicably, you could find a better solution—or simply feel lighter—within that inner space. Why do you think this happens to you so naturally? Think about the meaning of your silences...

I came to understand that silence is a space that allows the unseen to speak, the unknown to rise, and the sacred to be received. On the spiritual path, silence is not something we run from. It is something we learn to walk with.

Because in silence, we are no longer reacting. We are *receiving*. We are no longer performing—we are *present*. And in that presence, the guidance of the unseen can finally rise. Many people miss divine messages not because they are absent, but because they are drowned out.

Even as I write these words, I am sitting in silence—letting the energy of creativity flow through me. I am listening, not just with my mind, but with a deeper part of myself that reveals the stories I must tell and the information I must share. The words do not come from noise. They come from stillness. They emerge from a space within me that is quiet enough to receive instruction.

And as you are reading this book, you too are practicing silence. You are listening—not with your ears, but with something more subtle. Your eyes see the words, but your soul translates them. The part of you that is reading is not passive. It is engaged in interpretation, drawing meaning from what I have written and applying it to the rhythm of your own life and understanding. That is the silent dialogue between souls, the space where writer and reader meet in spirit.

Silence holds knowledge.

That is why two people can read the same sentence and understand it differently. Because what we receive from the written word is filtered through the inner voice that reads it.

On the spiritual path, silence is not just a place of rest, it is a place of revelation.

Silence is where purpose becomes clear. In a world filled with distractions and expectations, it is only in silence that we can hear the voice of our true calling. When we practice silence, we create space to reconnect with our inner guidance. It is through silence that we receive clarity, direction, and strength.

Many spiritual paths have honored silence as a bridge between the seen and the unseen.

In many Indigenous traditions, silence is the space before ceremony, the pause before counsel, the deep listening to land, ancestors, and Spirit. In Christian monastic life, for example, monks and nuns, especially in the Trappist tradition, observe what is called *the Great Silence*, speaking only when necessary, so their hearts can stay fixed on God. In Buddhism, during *Noble Silence* retreats, no one speaks. The purpose is to learn to see the mind without the noise it loves to create. In Hinduism, silence is discipline. Yogis and sages may retreat into months or years of wordlessness, conserving the energy usually spent in speech and directing it inward toward the Self.

Across cultures and centuries, silence is an

opening where truth can enter. Therefore, trusting the unseen is telling you this: Let us learn to pause sometimes. Let us learn to be silent sometimes. Let us learn to simply be—to breathe and be present. The connection to the unseen does not always require loud rituals or grand displays of devotion; sometimes, it is as simple as breathing and being silent.

Without understanding the power of silence in spirituality, we may confuse movement with progress and noise with truth. But with it, we align with ourselves, not through force but through inner knowing. And when clarity comes, gratitude is the first response that overflows. As the soul, when truly reconnected, silently gives thanks without needing a reason.

CHAPTER 18

EMBRACING THE FLOW OF GRATITUDE

"Where gratitude lives, the Unseen breathes, because faith needs no evidence to feel abundance."

Perhaps some of you, like me, were taught at an early age to say "thank you" whenever you received something—a gift, a compliment, a gesture. Parents and teachers in kindergarten and elementary school often emphasized this habit, training children to respond politely, as a way of showing good manners. But in those early years, "thank you" is often more of a sign of kindness than gratitude itself. We are taught the words before we understand the energy behind them. We say it out of politeness, and it becomes a reflex.

As we grow older, this reflex can remain a conditioned response rather than a conscious one. We continue to say "thank you," sometimes without even thinking, and yet true gratitude, as a vibration, as alignment can still feel far away. That is because gratitude is not only about courtesy, but awareness.

Some of us were not raised to say "thank you." Not because we were ungrateful, but because the language of gratitude was never spoken around us. It was not part of our programming. We were taught how to survive, how to stand tall in the face of adversity, how to armor up when life came swinging. There was no space for softness, no time to pause and reflect on blessings. Gratitude therefore felt foreign, like a luxury we could not afford in environments that demanded strength above all.

For many, showing appreciation felt like lowering the guard. As if saying "thank you" meant giving away power. And so, instead of practicing gratitude, we learned performance. We became who we had to be in order to stay safe, to be accepted, to make it through. We wore strength like a costume. We mastered the art of carrying burdens without making a sound. But here, right now, if this sounds like your story, I want to tell you that you do not need the mask anymore.

Honor the versions of you that survive, knowing that now it is time to let a softer truth rise. It is time to look at yourself with reverence. You made it. Through every twist, every wound, every silence that tried to swallow you. You are still here!

Take a breath and see yourself.

See the moments that forged you. The days you had to be your own protector. The nights when no one clapped for you, but you showed up anyway. These are not just memories; they are monuments. Evidence that you were never weak, only uncelebrated.

Now, let gratitude enter. Be proud of who you became, and even more, of who you are becoming. Gratitude does not make you smaller. It reveals how vast your journey truly was.

Be grateful for your becoming. For the quiet, steady power that no longer needs to shout to be felt. This too, is strength.

Embracing the Flow of Gratitude

Gratitude is the energetic return of presence. It is how we acknowledge the meaning behind a gesture, a word, a moment. It is not just kindness, it is consciousness. And often, the world confuses the two.

We can use kindness to express gratitude but gratitude is not kindness.

Kindness is an action, a gesture, often extended outward to others. But gratitude is an inner recognition, a moment of intentional awareness where we acknowledge that something has uplifted us. It is more than a feeling—it is an understanding. And that is what makes it such a powerful spiritual practice. Gratitude requires consciousness.

It invites us to pause, to become aware of what has been given, and to hold space for the meaning behind it.

This is why gratitude flows so naturally with faith—faith in the unseen, and faith in ourselves. Because both require awareness beyond the physical. Both ask us to perceive with our soul.

Sometimes, people can describe children as "ungrateful." But often, it is not ingratitude—it is simply that the child has not yet developed the awareness to understand the depth of what is being done for them. A parent may be working tirelessly to keep their child safe, nurtured, and protected. But until the child can perceive the weight of that effort, they cannot reflect it back as gratitude.

Because gratitude is not automatic. It is a result of understanding.

Sometimes, people will hold on, to a kind action, they once did for you, treating it as a form of emotional debt—something you must repay whenever they need a favor. It becomes a kind of *emotional blackmail.*

True gratitude is born from awareness, not obligation. It flows freely, without needing to be earned or repaid. But sometimes, acts of kindness are not given from a pure place—they are offered with unspoken expectations. When someone gives only to receive or reminds you of what they did as a way to gain control, it is no longer a gift—it becomes a transaction. This is an *emotional bargaining*. The real act of giving asks for nothing in return. It honors the moment, the gesture, and the soul behind it without attachment.

I remember a moment that taught me this in a very human way. There was a time, I used to feel a certain frustration whenever I held the door for someone and they walked through without saying "thank you." I would wonder, "How hard is it to say those two words? Why not acknowledge the gesture?"

But now, I see it differently.

Holding the door is part of *who I am*. It is my expression of respect. No one asked me to do it—not even the stranger I did it for. So, why expect something in return? If they thank me, it is welcome. If they do not, it is fine too. There is no debt in kindness, especially when the act is chosen freely.

If I am driving a friend or a family member, I will hold the car door for them as they enter—not as an act of chivalry, but because my father once taught me it was a matter of safety. When he would open the door for me, he explained that it was his way of making sure I was securely inside before he began driving. I carry that same gesture of care with me now. Whenever I am the driver—which means someone has trusted me to carry them safely—I open the door, ensure they are seated securely, and only then do I begin to drive. It is my way of showing care, and I do not expect anything in return.

If you are expecting appreciation for every kind gesture you offer, you are missing the essence of living truly free. As you read in the section about boundaries, every action must come from a place of freedom, peace, and non-expectation. If something stirs uneasy within you, it is not genuine. Do not do it. Your soul does not understand forced offerings. Do it, only when it can be freely given. When you are smiling even when nothing is received.

I now understand that gratitude is a response—not a requirement. It is born when awareness meets action. Without awareness, gratitude does not bloom. It simply passes by unnoticed.

Today, on my spiritual path, I no longer see life as random. And because of that, I live in the flow of gratitude. I choose to be intentionally thankful—not only for the things I see and understand, but also for the things I do not yet see or comprehend.

I am grateful when I give, when I receive, and for everything and everyone living around me—for every unfolding.

I also understand that many compare the world we live in to a jungle. A place where only the strongest survive. There are lions—bold, aggressive, dominant—and there are sheep the quiet, the gentle, the ones who move through life with tenderness. And somehow, the more genuine someone appears, the more they are seen as prey. Vulnerability is mistaken for weakness. Softness becomes a risk. And so, many choose to harden.

But here is what I have come to believe: the Unseen is not blind to any of this.

The invisible forces that shape our lives are

PISTIS: The Art of Trusting the Unseen

deeply conscious. They do not operate on surface appearances. They move through the heart. And the heart—your heart—is what matters most.

We live in a world of survival because we have been conditioned to wear masks. To perform. To suppress our intuition and silence our truth. We are taught to praise those who keep us asleep, those who lead from ego, those who manipulate the narrative to maintain their power.

That is why awakening is not just a spiritual act—it is a revolution of awareness.

When you are awake, when you are truly present, you no longer need to become the lion to survive. You do not need to roar to be respected. Because you have become the eye of the jungle. The one who sees. The one who moves with intention, with wisdom, with clarity. And that kind of presence changes everything.

The eye does not seek to dominate. It observes, it understands, and it waits for alignment.

So, do not be ashamed of your gentleness. Do not betray your heart to play someone else's game. The world may appear wild, but the Unseen is always in motion—guiding, protecting, elevating those who dare to live with truth.

And in that truth, you are no longer a lion or a sheep. You are the vision that rises above them both.

I remember visiting the countryside in Haiti with my aunt, who worked for a French organization at this time. She used to bring me along to some training as a helper. At the time, I noticed how fresh the air felt. The trees looked young and alive. The land breathed differently.

And there, I saw something I had never seen before: gratitude for nature. One man once told me: "We must be grateful for the river, the trees,

Embracing the Flow of Gratitude

the rain, and the sun—because without them, we cannot exist."

At the time, I did not fully grasp his words. My life was different. But now, with deeper awareness, I carry his wisdom differently. Because he was right:

If the trees disappear;
If the rivers dry up;
If the rain stops falling;
And the Sun ceases to shine;
Life itself begins to fade.

And yet, we often forget to say thank you to the very things that sustain us. The plants that give us oxygen. The sun that warms us. The waters that nourish the land. They have been holding the door open for us, day after day. And most of the time, we just pass through—unaware, unconscious...

Now that I understand that everything is connected, and because I am aware, I have become more grateful.

Gratitude does not need to start with the big miracles, but with the small, sacred things that keep us alive—often unnoticed.

"Give thanks in all circumstances; for this is God's will for you."
—1 Thessalonians 5:18 (NIV)

The flow of gratitude is a lifestyle.

It is the conscious decision to live with reverence—to be thankful not only for what is around you, but also for what is within you. It is the choice to walk through each moment with awareness, knowing that every season of your life is guiding you closer to your essence—and by extension, to the Divine Source itself. For that alone, you give thanks. Gratitude, in this sense, is not just a response. It is a way of seeing.

It is the ability to understand that when someone expresses genuine gratitude—not as flattery, not as manipulation, but from a place of true awareness—it creates a ripple. It awakens a feeling of appreciation, even when no expectation was attached to the act.

And just as humans can feel that appreciation, so can everything else. The trees, the waters, the winds, and the energies that live around us—all respond to our awareness. Because everything that is alive is connected to vibration. And gratitude is one of the highest frequencies we can embody.

Gratitude, when practiced intentionally, becomes a rhythm woven into our daily life. It does not need to be loud or public. It can be a silent "thank you" when you wake up, as simple as placing your hand over your heart during a moment of stillness. Some people keep a gratitude journal; others offer a prayer before meals or smile toward the sky. These small acts are not about routine, they are about *understanding*. They are the *knowing* of what is already present. *Knowing* that, even in the middle of uncertainty, something good still exists.

The Parable of the Hidden Seeds

There was once a woman who inherited a small piece of land from her grandmother. It was rocky, dry, and overlooked by others in the village. Most people said nothing would grow there. Still, the woman accepted the land with quiet reverence. Her grandmother had whispered to her once, "Everything sacred begins with the unseen."

She began to clear the land—not in haste, but

with intention. She removed the stones, softened the soil, and watered it daily, though nothing yet had been planted. The neighbors watched in confusion.

"You are wasting your time," they said.

"There is nothing there."

"No promise. No harvest. Just dirt."

But the woman smiled and kept tending the earth. Every evening, she sat in silence and thanked the land as if it had already bloomed. She whispered words of blessing over the soil, even though it was still bare. To her, it was not empty—it was sacred waiting.

One morning, a storm came. Not violent, but steady. Rain soaked the ground for hours. And when the sun returned days later, something began to stir. Tiny green shoots broke through the soil—sprouts she had never planted herself.

Unseen by her, long ago, her grandmother had hidden seeds deep in the earth—seeds that only revealed themselves when the time, the care, and the rain had all aligned.

✦ ✦ ✦

There will be days when gratitude feels far away. When grief, confusion, or exhaustion fogs your vision. It is okay. Gratitude is not denial. It is not forcing a smile when your heart aches. Rather, it is finding one small light in the middle of the dark.

When we choose to live in the flow of gratitude, we align ourselves with abundance, peace, and joy—not because we are forcing life to give us more, but because we are finally awake enough to see that we were already surrounded by more than enough.

PISTIS: The Art of Trusting the Unseen

Gratitude transforms our state from seeking to receiving. From resistance to flow. From surviving to truly living.

"Let us rise up and be thankful, for if we didn't learn a lot today, at least we learned a little... If we didn't gain anything, at least we didn't lose anything."
—Buddha

CHAPTER 19

WHEN THE SPIRIT LEADS

To me, *spirit* is this part of me that I am *knowing*.

It is the force that has walked with me through every silence I did not know how to explain. Spirit is the part of me that cannot be broken. The part that knew who I was long before the world gave me a name or an identity. It is the inner compass that still points north, even when everything around me feels uncertain.

There were seasons in life when logic could not carry me. When every choice I was taught to make feels misaligned. When the paths I planned began to disappear and I was left with nothing but silence, breath, and a strange kind of knowing.

It is in those moments that I have learned to listen—not to my fears, not to my doubts—but to the voice of the unseen. The voice *within.*

At first, I have not always understood the reasons. Sometimes I questioned the timing, resisted the direction, and even cried when I had to let go of what I thought I needed. But every time I chose to trust the unseen, something in me expanded.

Even in the absence of clarity, I felt held. Even when I had no answers, I felt movement.

There was a time when I followed every rule that was expected of me. I made plans. I created structures. I told myself I had figured it out. And then life... interrupted. A diagnosis. A pain I could not schedule. A silence I could not escape.

I remember sometimes, lying in pains, unable to move, unable to speak, with nothing but my breath and a faint awareness that I was not alone. It was always something deeper. Something that reminded me to never let go of myself, while teaching me to let go of control.

Then, I started to understand when my spirit leads. I started to understand how to merge my body, soul and higher mind.

I became less afraid to ask for help when I needed it. To call upon my spirit when guidance was necessary—or simply when I needed to feel *present*. I called on the spirit of focus, of creativity, of blessing, and of gratitude, as they all live in me. I asked to be taught. I asked for revelation.

The first lesson was always this: remove the armor and embrace yourself fully.

At one point, I questioned whether the voices guiding me were Christian, even if all the teachings were about loving myself and loving one another. Because there were so many ideologies about how the divine could communicate; I was still, in a way, programmed to believe more in what was told to me than in what I was experiencing. But then, came the clarity that I was born with my consciousness. And what kind of Divine force would give us awareness, only to demand that we abandon it?

Awareness is a gift. With it, we become more ourselves; and by becoming more ourselves, we come closer to the Divine within us. So, pay attention to any teaching, any voice, any instruction that asks you to dim your light.

Most of the time, by asking for guidance, I would not receive a full map. I receive one step. And then another. Thus, I understood that is how

When the Spirit Leads

the spirit moves—it does not always give the whole vision. Because you are participating in every step of your life. It brings you awareness and clarity. Then a vibration that matches your rhythm of understanding.

Sometimes, it reveals itself after you set your boundaries and let go of what no longer serves you. Which means, every time you make space by truly choosing yourself in an act of love, you give permission to your spirit to walk with you.

I was taught to pray like this: *"God, please give me wisdom and strength [...]"* But now, my conversation has changed. I say: *"I am calling upon the wisdom and strength that have already been divinely given to me—gifts that live within me. I now choose to connect with this part of myself and allow it to guide me."*

I have come to understand that it is not always necessary to ask for what you already possess. Affirming and knowing that it belongs to you is the key to the Divine—and to the faith (*pistis*) that has already been offered to you. The sacred work is to connect with what is already within you, to name it, to communicate with it, to align with it. And from that place of inner union, you can offer your gratitude to the Higher Force of the Universe—the Source from which your awareness flows, the presence that sustains and protects all beings.

The unity that I now feel in myself had led me to places my intellect would have rejected. To say yes to paths that had no guarantees. To meet people I did not expect and release attachments I thought I needed.

By seeing how Spirit leads, I have come to understand that faith is not something that is teachable. I believe it can only be experienced.

Even if explained in testimonies, it does not live in textbooks and certainly has no secret recipe or

PISTIS: The Art of Trusting the Unseen

religion. Because faith is not a doctrine. It is not confined to temples, churches, or sacred texts. It is a movement of the soul. A recognition that something greater than you exists, even if you cannot name it, touch it, or explain it. Faith is what rises when your plans fall apart and something within you still chooses to trust.

Some people find trust through religion, and that is beautiful. But faith itself is not born from religion. It existed long before labels. Long before systems. Long before division.

You can have faith without ever belonging to a specific tradition—and still walk more closely with the Divine than someone who recites sacred words without presence.

It is felt. It is lived. It is earned through every step you take into the unknown, and every time you listen to your inner voice when the world tells you otherwise. Faith, in its purest form, is a relationship between your soul and the unseen.

That kind of intimacy cannot be taught because, truly—it does not grow from logic. Because if you are waiting for everything to make sense before you move, you will never take the first step. And—if you desire the supernatural to unfold in your life, you must begin to move as one who *is* supernatural. You must act in rhythm with a force that is greater than explanation.

Perhaps you have done it before.

You may not call it Spirit. You may not even have a name for it—and that is completely fine. We are all influenced by different cultures, different beliefs, different languages. The name is not what matters. What matters is the *knowing*. The *feeling*...

Have you ever felt guided by something beyond logic? Have you ever known something without knowing how you knew? If so, then you have already walked with Spirit—whether you knew it or not. Because Spirit does not need permission to speak. It only needs your attention. It does not belong to any one religion or name. It belongs to you. It is part of your design, and you are already living the mystery. Now, the invitation is simply to trust it more.

I have met people along my path who could not comprehend my way of thinking. People who do not believe in anything higher than themselves. But even that, I have come to respect it, knowing that we are learning different lessons in this lifetime. As I also come to understand that if you truly believe in yourself—*fully*—with clarity, intention, and reverence, then you have already tasted the essence of faith and therefore walking with the unseen even unconsciously.

For me, I can speak of my spirit with conviction because I have lived the experiences that shaped my knowing. I have followed my inner voice when no logic supported it, and it led me to peace.

I walked away from things I thought I needed and found something better waiting. I have been held in moments when no one else was there.

I have been guided when no map existed.

So, my faith is not merely belief. It is understanding. It is consciousness. It is the sacred knowing that something is always present—always holding me, always aware.

Perhaps the greatest lesson I continue to learn is to respect everything I understand—and everything I *do not*. Because both are sacred. And both are part of the unfolding.

Across centuries, continents, and teachings, spiritual voices have debated the subject of what it means to know, to believe, to remember, to feel connected to the Source. Therefore, I will not attempt to define what has already been named a thousand ways.

But I will say this: *"When Spirit leads, it will not always explain itself. And in time, you will understand why the step you thought of taking in the dark was the moment you began to walk in your truth. Because when you walk in your truth, you do not just follow destiny— you begin to shape it. This is where free will begins to dance."*

CHAPTER 20

THE DANCE BETWEEN DESTINY AND FREE WILL

You are not a puppet of fate—you are a partner in creation. Yes, I said it.

I began the introduction of this book by saying: "If you feel guided [...]." One may ask: "if we are guided—if the soul has a mission and a purpose—does the human truly have free will? If the path is divinely led, can we ever genuinely stray? These questions have echoed through temples and stirred the hearts of mystics and philosophers for centuries.

We begin to question because there are moments in life when everything feels already written—the people we meet, the turns we take, the pain we endure, the peace that follows. It is as if an unseen force has charted the course long before our first breath. And in those moments, we may wonder: was this always meant to happen? Did I ever really have a choice?

To respond to this, let me return to a metaphor I offered earlier about your homeland sending you on a mission to a foreign land. Or, to make it more familiar: imagine your parents ask you to take their car and go to the grocery store to buy a few specific things.

Now, even though you have accepted the task,

your free will remains completely intact.

You can choose to go straight to the store and buy exactly what they asked. You can decide to lie and say some items were out of stock—even if they weren't. You might stop to see friends along the way and still complete the task. Or, you can take the car and completely abandon the original assignment—doing something entirely your own.

The choice is yours.

But—and this is essential to understand—every choice sets something into motion. Every action creates a reaction. And because nothing is ever truly lost, but only transformed—that reaction will begin to reshape your perception of the task, of yourself, and of your journey. In the end, whatever your choice may have been, what you will always find is learning.

> *"For every action, there is an equal and opposite reaction."*
> —Isaac Newton.

> *"Every action has a consequence."*
> —The Law of Karma in Hinduism and Buddhism.

That is why, at times, it feels as though our past has shaped our present, and our present choices are already shaping our future. This is the dance—where actions create reactions, and unfolding transformations allow us to see ourselves more clearly and learn through our freedom.

> *"Nothing is lost, nothing is created, everything is transformed."*
> —Antoine Lavoisier

The Dance Between Destiny and Free Will

We often hear the phrase: "Practice makes perfect." And while it may sound like a cliché, there is wisdom in it—not only for our careers or craft, but for our spiritual path as well.

In the physical world, the more you learn a skill, the more confident and fluent you become. You no longer fumble through the motions—you move with grace and ease.

The same principle applies to the soul, as spiritual alignment is also a skill.

The more you learn—not just intellectually, but soulfully—the more aware you become of the meaning behind your actions. You begin to notice how certain thoughts shift your energy, how certain choices ripple beyond the moment. Your life becomes more intentional, more rooted in clarity. You no longer react by habit—you respond from wisdom.

Each day, you grow more attuned to the subtle voice within. Each choice becomes an act of remembrance. And again, with time, you realize that alignment is not about being flawless. It is about being aware.

The more aware you are, the more naturally your life begins to reflect your purpose. Not because you are trying to be perfect, but because you are practicing presence—and presence always leads you home.

This practice of connecting with yourself is what gives birth to guidance.

Guidance is not control. It does not remove your free will. It does not override your choices. Rather, it arises from alignment.

The more you know yourself—not the version shaped by the world, but the version remembered through your spirit—the clearer the inner signals become. You start sensing when something feels off, even if it looks right.

You recognize when a door is truly meant for you, and when it is just a distraction dressed in opportunity.

This is the space where guidance flows. Not as a command, but as a *knowing*. Not as force, but as a frequency of peace.

You still choose—always. But your choices begin to align more easily with your soul's truth, because you are no longer guessing with uncertainty. You start living in the freedom of who you truly are.

When people say they are "being guided," what they often mean is this: "I have reached a level of connection with myself so deep that my spirit recognizes what resonates with my path and I choose to follow it."

That is not a loss of freedom. That is the highest form of freedom to choose in harmony with your true self.

Some might still ask: "But what if, even if it seems like we are in control, we are actually just puppets of destiny? What if everything is already shaped—and we are simply following the script?"

It is a valid question. But here is what I believe, from my soul to yours: you are not a puppet. You are a seed.

The seed of an oak tree contains the potential for great roots, wide branches, and shade for generations to come. But how fast it grows, how tall it rises, how strong it becomes—all depends on the conditions, choices, and care it receives.

The potential is there. The path is possible. But the outcome is shaped in relationship between your spirit and your choice.

Yes, I believe there are divine patterns shaping us—but we are never passive in that shaping. Our responses matter. Our courage matters. Even our

The Dance Between Destiny and Free Will

"mistakes" matter.

You are being guided, yes—but not manipulated. You are being shaped, yes—but not subdued.

You are becoming—and that becoming requires your participation, and most of it—your knowledge of yourself.

Let's take the principle of manifestation as a tool to understand this even more clearly.

The very fact that you have the ability to create, reshape, transform, and call into existence something that does not yet exist in the physical—is proof that you are not a prisoner of destiny. You are a participant in it. You are a creator.

Manifestation is a spiritual expression of free will. It is your soul saying, "I choose," and all the unseen laws around you responding, "So it shall be."

If you were merely a puppet, you would not have this power. But you do.

Now, some might ask me: "Would you say you were destined to follow a spiritual path? Because based on your stories, it seems like you were pushed at a very young age to experience spiritual events—and now, after years of burying them, you have no choice but to follow."

To that I say: "Yes, I was called. But I am not forced."

What you are witnessing is alignment, not coercion. What looks like a controlled destiny is remembrance returning.

I did not lose my free will, I found *my* truth. I chose to listen. I chose to say yes. And that, to me, is the most powerful use of free will: to choose my soul, again and again.

You are not here to be controlled. You are here to awaken. And when you remember who you truly are, your choices begin to reflect that truth. Not because you must, but because your spirit would accept nothing less.

To help you understand my thoughts, let's imagine that before you entered this life, your soul chose a melody—a divine song uniquely yours. It holds your essence, your gifts, your mission, and the rhythm of your becoming. But the way you play it is entirely up to you.

You can play it slowly, hesitantly... or with fire and passion. You can even silence it altogether, pretending it was never there. But the melody remains. It does not leave you. It waits. And the moment you begin to hum its tune again, even faintly, something shifts. Clarity returns. The air around you vibrate. Not because you are being rewarded—but because you are in resonance.

You are not forced to play the song of your soul. But the moment you do... you begin to remember who you are.

In ancient Kemet, from the Book of the Dead, the soul's heart was weighed against the feather of Ma'at—truth, balance, and divine order; not to determine if one had been controlled by destiny, but to reflect how one had chosen to walk in alignment. The judgment was not on fate—it was on choice.

I shared this example to illustrate how choices were viewed in ancient Kemet, but personally, I no longer believe in judgment—I believe in learning. I am not imposing this belief on anyone. This is simply my understanding, shaped by my own path.

For me, no true master—no being genuinely devoted to teaching you—will also judge you, or threaten to burn you for eternity. The voices that guide me do not preach fear. They speak of growth, of awareness, of returning to truth—not

The Dance Between Destiny and Free Will

punishment.

Have you ever wondered why some of you feel comfortable with the idea of being punished? Why so many of us have internalized suffering as something deserved—perhaps even divine? How has it become so natural for some of us to accept—and sometimes even expect—that those who are different from us should die and suffer for eternity?

Have you ever gone back—not just to the scriptures, but to the translations? To the original language? To the cultural context in which certain verses were written, spoken, and interpreted?

Because I believe that sometimes, what we fear is not the Divine—it is the version of the Divine we were handed.

A version filtered through empire, through power, through centuries of control. A version that taught obedience through fear rather than love through awareness. And yet, deep within you, there may still be a voice that questions: *Does the Divine really need to judge and burn me if I do something that I do not truly understand?*

I do not believe so.

Because *truth* does not require fear to be powerful. It carries its own resonance. It awakens, not with threat, but with light.

So again, I return to this: The Spirit within me does not shame. The Divine does not threaten to burn if obedience is not met. The voices within teach. They reveal. They expand. They remind me that I am not here to be punished. I am here to remember who I am.

> *"The lips of wisdom are closed, except to the ears of understanding."*
> —The Kybalion

PISTIS: The Art of Trusting the Unseen

One must choose to seek. Each of us has the free will to ask for guidance—or to walk away from it.

"Thus, I have explained to you this knowledge that is more secret than all secrets. Ponder over it deeply, and then do as you wish."
—Bhagavad Gita 18:63

CHAPTER 21

THE RETURN TO LIGHT

You have walked with me through memory, silence, revelation, and resistance, and now we arrive here—not at an end, but at a return. A return to the mindfulness that was always within you. A return to trusting the unseen.

You were never reading only my words. You were also reading yourself. You were experiencing what you already carried: the stillness and the understanding.

You are not what happened to you. You are not only the name the world gave you. You are not the role you had to play to survive. You are consciousness disguised in form; spirit wrapped in memory, awakened through presence.

All throughout this book, I never asked you to agree with me. I asked you to listen—not to me, but to the voice within you. The quiet one. The unseen one. The one that speaks when everything else grows still.

That voice will not always give you answers. Sometimes, it will only give you awareness; and that awareness will become the soil from which everything else will grow.

This is the way of *Pistis*. It is not belief alone, but trust; not blind faith, but conscious alignment; and not performance, but presence.

This journey was not about becoming

something new. It was about coming home to what was never lost.

There will be days you forget. Days when fear returns wearing a familiar face. Days when the path feels distant and silence feels like abandonment. On those days, I want you to remember this: *The Divine never stopped speaking.*

The language of the unseen is not always words. It is resonance. It is the way your chest expands when truth enters. It is the way peace settles when something is real. It is the way your spirit softens when you are aligned.

Yes, you may have wandered. You may have doubted. You may have forgotten the sound of your own soul's voice. But now—you begin to remember. And that remembrance is the beginning of everything.

Do not expect thunder. Trust the whisper.

Do not wait for permission. Honor the pulse within. You are not waiting to be chosen. You already were.

You are not a follower. You are not a copy. You are a voice. A melody. A soul designed with divine precision.

No matter what you do next, walk with your spirit aligned. Breathe with your soul awake.

I believe that the world does not need more noise. It needs more remembrance. More beings who trust the unseen and still choose to walk with open hearts.

There is no final chapter. Only the one you now write with your choices, your presence, your peace.

You are the message. You are the unfolding miracle. Walk forward not as someone who "knows it all," but as someone who listens deeper. Trust the unseen. Speak to the silence and let life speak back.

When in doubt, return to this:

The Return to Light

"I am spirit clothed in form, walking this planet for a purpose greater than I can see. I trust that my path is aligned not only with my highest good, but with the unfolding of all. I carry light—not as something I shine, but as something I remember."

Perhaps now, it makes more sense why I describe myself this way.

This is not the end. This is your sacred return.

PISTIS: The Art of Trusting the Unseen

EPILOGUE

If you made it here, you did not just read this book, you walked a path. One that began not on page one, but perhaps long before that—in a question, a moment of silence, or a forgotten dream.

May the light you have touched here not just inspire you but remind you to trust that it was always yours.

With love and remembrance,
—Samanda Leroy

ACKNOWLEDGMENTS

To walk the path of writing this book was to walk a path of remembrance, of my own voice, my spirit, my wounds, and of the thread that runs through all things. I did not walk alone.

To the forces, seen and unseen, whose whispers carried me when I had no words—thank you. Your presence lives on these pages.

To my family, whose stories live inside of mine—thank you for being the soil where my earliest roots were planted, and for teaching me that silence, laughter, and even pain can be sacred teachers.

To the friends who held space for me—whether in conversation, stillness, or shared tears—thank you for being mirrors of compassion when I could not yet see my reflection clearly.

To every soul I have met in this lifetime—the ones who, consciously or unconsciously, became my teachers, and those whose lives I have also transformed—thank you. Each encounter has shaped me into this becoming. Each lesson has carved depth into my path. For every crossing, I am forever grateful.

To the guides—spiritual and human—who reminded me to trust the unknown, to rest in the pause, and to speak when truth trembled through me—thank you for walking with integrity.

To every soul who will pick up this book and feel less alone, more seen, more whole—thank you. This book is as much yours as it is mine.

And finally, to the Divine Light—however it chooses to reveal itself in our lives—thank you for never leaving, even when we forget to look.

With deep gratitude,
—Samanda Leroy

ABOUT THE AUTHOR

Samanda Leroy is a spiritual writer, intuitive scholar, and lifelong seeker of *her truth*. Her work explores space where we meet the Divine—where pain becomes transformation, silence becomes wisdom, and memory becomes a guide.

Born with a deep curiosity for the unseen, Samanda has spent her life listening to the quiet spaces most overlooked. From childhood visions to adult awakenings, she has walked a path marked by questions that do not always have answers, and revelations that come when least expected.

Through her writing, she invites others to reconnect with their own inner wisdom. She believes healing is not about fixing what is broken but remembering what has always been whole.

This book, as a guided journey, is not her first step—but it may be your invitation to begin. Her words serve as a reminder that you are already who you have been searching for.

REFERENCES AND RECOMMENDED READING

The books, videos referenced, and recommended reading here are not part of any paid promotion or affiliate partnership. I do not receive compensation of any kind for sharing them.

These works are simply a reflection of the voices, teachings, and insights that found their way to me during the period of my spiritual transition. Some referenced ideologies I had long carried in silence; others offered language for what had only been felt. I share them as companions on the path of exploration, intended to support your spiritual curiosity and understanding.

Some works appear in both the *Book References* and *Recommended Reading* sections for deeper exploration.

BOOK REFERENCES:

Allen, James P. *Genesis in Egypt: The Philosophy of Ancient Egyptian Creation Accounts*. New Haven: Yale Egyptological Seminar, 1988.

Allen, James P., trans. *The Ancient Egyptian Pyramid Texts*. Atlanta: Society of Biblical Literature, 2005.Bohm, David. *Wholeness and the Implicate*

Order. London: Routledge, 1980.

Easwaran, Eknath, trans. *The Bhagavad Gītā*. Tomales, CA: Nilgiri Press, 2007.

Easwaran, Eknath, trans. *The Upanishads*. Tomales, CA: Nilgiri Press, 2007.

Hermes Trismegistus. *The Emerald Tablet of Hermes*. Translated by Dennis W. Hauck. Newburyport, MA: Weiser Books, 2004.

Holy Bible: New International Version. Colorado Springs: Biblica, 2011.

Jung, Carl G. *The Collected Works of C. G. Jung*. Vol. 9, Pt. 1, *The Archetypes and the Collective Unconscious*. 2nd ed. Bollingen Series XX. Princeton, NJ: Princeton University Press, 1968.

Lao Tzu. *Tao Te Ching: A New English Version*. Translated by Stephen Mitchell. New York: Harper Perennial Modern Classics, 2006.

Mandukya Upanishad. Translated by Swami Nikhilananda. Madras: Sri Ramakrishna Math, 1949.

Meyer, Marvin, ed. *The Nag Hammadi Scriptures*. New York: HarperOne, 2007.

Obenga, Théophile. *The Shabaka Stone: An Introduction*. Paris: Présence Africaine, 2004.

Radhakrishnan, S., trans. "Mandūkya Upaniṣad." In *The Principal Upanishads*, 708–714. New Delhi: Indus, 1994.

References and Recommended Reading

Rumi. *The Essential Rumi*. Translated by Coleman Barks, with John Moyne, A. J. Arberry, and Reynold Nicholson. San Francisco: HarperSanFrancisco, 1995.

Silva, José, and Philip Miele. *The Silva Mind Control Method*. New York: Pocket Books, 1977.

Smith, Danita. *The Shabaka Stone and the Memphite Theology*. BLACKandEducation.org, 2023. http://BLACKandEducation.org.

Suzuki, Daisetz T., trans. *The Laṅkāvatāra Sūtra*. Delhi: Motilal Banarsidass, 1999.

The Egyptian Book of the Dead. Translated by E. A. Wallis Budge. Edited by John Baldock. London: Sirius Publishing, 2024.

Three Initiates. *The Kybalion: A Study of the Hermetic Philosophy of Ancient Egypt and Greece*. Chicago: The Yogi Publication Society, 1908.

VIDEOS REFERENCES

Cambridge University Press. *The Yoruba from Prehistory to the Present*. YouTube video, 1:12:24. Posted October 21, 2020.
https://www.youtube.com/watch?v=fRy92OJCtcY.

Kosinec, Tony. *Kabbalah Revealed with Tony Kosinec – Full Course*. YouTube video, 6:07:55. Published by KabbalahInfo, May 1, 2019.
https://www.youtube.com/watch?v=NkvITHLbNhw

Missler, Chuck. *Kabbalah and the Rise of Mysticism – Session 1 – Chuck Missler*. YouTube video, 54:34.

Published by Koinonia House, August 16, 2022.
https://youtu.be/8ngtLHGRw7I

Navajo Traditional Teachings. *Walk in Beauty... The Purpose of Life | Navajo Teachings.* YouTube video, 7:14. Published on January 24, 2022.
https://www.youtube.com/watch?v=EP4_lDph2io
(Also visit navajotraditionalteachings.com)

NASA. *Cosmic Dawn (NASA+ Original Documentary).* YouTube video, 1:36:45. Published by Nasa, on June 11, 2025.
https://www.youtube.com/watch?v=uSMGENDH_QI

Proctor, Bob. *Do You Know Who You Are?* YouTube video, 23:06. Published by Proctor Gallagher Institute, on May 14, 2015.
https://www.youtube.com/watch?v=E44kFkyl_Y8

The Kybalion. Directed by Ronni Thomas. Featuring Mitch Horowitz, Paula Roberts, and Daniel Ryan. Documentary. 2022. 1:00:15.
https://geni.us/WatchTheKybalion

Thompson, George. *Taoism (Daoism) Explained by Taoist Master.* YouTube video, 5:56. Published on December 8, 2017.
https://www.youtube.com/watch?v=kij4kKSGzCE

References and Recommended Reading

RECOMMENDED READING:

- Allen, James P. *Genesis in Egypt: The Philosophy of Ancient Egyptian Creation Accounts.*
- Coelho, Paulo. *The Alchemist.*
- Goddard, Neville. *The Neville Collection.*
- Hadsell, Helene. *In Contact with Other Realms.*
- Hanh, Thich Nhat. *The Heart of the Buddha's Teaching.*
- Jung, Carl G. *The Symbolic Life.*
- Kuo-Deemer, Mimi. *Qigong and the Tai Chi Axis.*
- Laozi. *Tao Te Ching.* Translated by Stephen Mitchell.
- Lin, Chunyi. *Born a Healer.*
- Maharshi, Ramana. *Be As You Are: The Teachings of Sri Ramana Maharshi.*
- Murphy, Joseph. *The Power of Your Subconscious Mind.*
- Pagels, Elaine. *The Gnostic Gospels.*
- Peale, Norman Vincent. *The Power of Positive Thinking.*
- Proctor, Bob. *You Were Born Rich.*
- Scovel Shinn, Florence. *The Game of Life and How to Play It.*
- Shakya, Sumitra. *The Path to Inner Peace.*
- Silva, José, and Philip Miele. *The Silva Mind Control Method.*
- Somé, Malidoma Patrice. *Of Water and the Spirit: Ritual, Magic, and Initiation in the Life of an African Shaman.*
- Suzuki, D.T., trans. *Laṅkāvatāra Sūtra.*
- Three Initiates. *The Kybalion.*
- Yogananda, Paramahansa. *Autobiography of a Yogi.*
- Yogananda, Paramahansa. *The Yoga of Jesus.*

www.ingramcontent.com/pod-product-compliance
Lightning Source LLC
Chambersburg PA
CBHW032040150426
43194CB00006B/359